WOMAN'S CIRCLE

Credits: Text by S. Golin
H. Applefield

Cover Design - Barbara Baron 1994

Copyright © 1994 P.S.I. & Associates, Inc.
1994 Edition

P.S.I. & Associates, Inc.
13322 S.W. 128th Street
Miami, Florida 33186
(305) 255-7959

ISBN #1-55993-278-3

29004

TABLE OF CONTENTS

WHERE TO FIND...

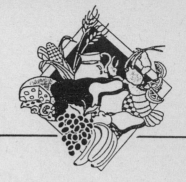

1 HELPFUL HINTS
& TIPS

ABBREVIATIONS

tsp ....teaspoon
tbsp ....tablespoon
c ....cup
pt..pint
qt......................................quarter
oz.....................................ounce
fl. oz.....................fluid ounce

doz................................dozen
med............................medium
min..............................minute
hr. ....hour
sq...............................square
pkg. ....package
lb. ....pound

OVEN TEMPERATURES

Very slow ....250°
Slow..................................300°
Moderate ....325-350°
Moderately hot ....375°
Hot ....400-425°
Very hot ....450-500°

All temperatures are Fahrenheit.

HOW TO MEASURE

Dash ....less than 1/8 tsp.
3 tsp. ....1 tbs.
4 tbs. ....1/4 cup
5 1/3 tbs. ....1/3 cup
8 tbs. ....1/2 cup
10 2/3 tbs. ....2/3 cup
12 tbs. ....3/4 cup
16 tbs............................1 cup
1 cup ....8 oz.
1 cup..........................1/2 pint
2 cups ....1 pint
2 pints ....1 quart
4 cups ....1 quart
4 quarts.......................1 gallon
8 quarts ....1 peck
4 pecks.......................1 bushel
2 tbs...........................1 liq. oz.
16 oz...........................1 pound

GUIDE FOR NUMBER OF SERVINGS

Vegetables and Side Dishes
Allow a minimum of half cup per serving.

Meat, Poultry and Fish
Roasts, stewing meat, veal chops and steaks: 1 lb. with bone serves 2, one lb. boneless serves 3.

Lamb chops, steak, spare ribs, poultry: allow 3/4 lb. per serving.

Hamburger, liver and fish: one pound serves 3.

Always allow for second helpings. The quantities given are for adult portion. One adult portion will generally serve 2 children.

5

SUBSTITUTES

1 whole egg	=	2 yolks,
or	=	1 Tablespoon plain egg-based salad dressing

1 cup brown sugar	=	1 cup white sugar plus 4 Tablespoons molasses

1 cup butter	=	7/8 cup rendered fat,
or	=	1 cup hydrogenated fat
or	=	7/8 cup solid vegetable shortening plus 1/2 teaspoon salt

(to measure 7/8 cup, measure one cup then remove 2 Tbsp)

1 square chocolate	=	3 Tablespoons cocoa and 1 Tablespoon oil

(this makes 1 ounce of unsweetened chocolate)

1 cup corn syrup	=	1 cup sugar plus 1/4 cup water or other liquid called for in recipe

1 Tablespoons flour	=	1 Tablespoon cornstarch,
or	=	1 Tablespoon rice starch,
or	=	1 Tablespoon arrowroot,
or	=	2 Tablespoons instant mashed potatoes,
or	=	2 Tablespoons cornmeal,
or	=	2 Tablespoons quick-cooking tapioca

(for thickening gravy or sauce)

1 cup sour milk	=	1 cup sweet milk with one of the following:

        1 Tablespoon vinegar
        1 Tablespoon lemon juice
        1 3/4 teaspoon cream of tartar

1 cup cake flour	=	7/8 cup all-purpose flour

Others:

Bread Crumbs — Use finely crushed corn flakes,
      or — any unsweetened cereal,
      or — crushed potato flakes,
      or — instant mashed potatoes

Ketchup — combine 1 cup tomato sauce or mashed canned tomatoes, 1-1/4 cups brown sugar, 2 Tablespoons vinegar, 1/4 teaspoon cinnamon and a dash of clove and allspice.

SUBSTITUTIONS

USE:	FOR:
1 cup less 3 Tbs. shortening	1 cup butter
3 Tbs. cocoa plus 1.2 tsp. oil	1 oz. unsweetened chocolate
2 egg yolks	1 whole egg (in baking)
2 Tbs. flour	1 Tbs. cornstarch
7/8 cup (1 cup less 2 Tbs.) unsifted all-purpose flour	1 cup sifted all-purpose flour
7/8 cup (1 cup less 2 Tbs.) sifted all-purpose flour	1 cup sifted cake flour
1 Tbs. lemon juice or vinegar plus enough milk to make 1 cup	1 cup sour milk or buttermilk
1/2 cup evaporated milk plus 1/2 cup water	1 cup fresh milk
1 cup brown sugar, packed	1 cup granulated sugar
1/2 cup maple syrup plus 1/4 cup corn syrup, and reduce liquid by 1/4 cup	1 cup granulated sugar
1 cup honey plus 1/4 to 1/2 tsp. baking soda, and reduce liquid by 1/4 cup	1 cup granulated sugar
3/4 cup sugar plus 1/4 cup liquid	1 cup honey
1 tsp. instant soup mix plus 1 cup boiling water	1 cup bullion

7

COMMON FOOD EQUIVALENTS

Bread crumbs	3 oz.	1 cup
Butter or shortening	1 lb.	2 cups
Cheese	1 lb.	4 cups grated
Chocolate	1 oz.	4 cups grated
Coconut (shredded)	1 lb.	6 cups
Cottage cheese	1 lb.	2 cups
Cream cheese	3 oz. pkg.	6-2/3 Tablespoons
Eggs (whole)	4-6	1 cup
Eggs (white)	8-10	1 cup
Eggs (yolk)	12-14	1 cup
Flour:		
All Purpose	1 lb.	4 cups unsifted
Cake	1 lb.	4-1/2 cups unsifted
Whole Wheat	1 lb.	4 cups
Marshmallows	1 lb.	4 cups (64)
Raisins	1 lb.	2 cups packed
Rice	1 lb.	2 cups uncooked, or 6 cups cooked
Sugar:		
Brown	1 lb.	2 cups packed
Confectioners	1 lb.	4 cups sifted
Granulated	1 lb.	2 cups
Whipping Cream	1/2 pint	2 cups whipped

FOOD EQUIVALENTS

APPLES
    1 pound   3 medium (3 cups sliced)

BUTTER (and other fats)
    1 lb.   2 cups
    1/2 lb.   1 cup
    1/4 lb.   1/2 cup

CHEESE
    1 lb. cottage cheese   2 cups
    8 oz. pkg. cottage cheese   1 cup
    8 oz. pkg. cream cheese   1 cup (1/2 lb.)
    1 lb. Amer. or Cheddar   3-4 cups grated

CHOCOLATE (unsweetened)
    1 square   1 oz. or 1 tbs. when melted
    1/2 lb.   8 - 1 oz. squares

COFFEE
    1 lb.   80 tbs. (40 servings)

CREAM
    1/2 pint coffee cream   6-8 servings of cream
    1/2 pint (1 cup) whipping (OR   2 cups when whipped
    1 pkg. dessert topping)

DATES
    1 lb. whole   1 1/2 - 1 3/4 cups pitted and cut up

EGGS
    5 whole eggs   1 cup
    8-10 egg whites   1 cup
    12-14 egg yolks   1 cup

FOOD EQUIVALENTS

FLOUR
1 lb. all-purpose	4 cups, sifted
1 lb. cake & pastry flour	4-1/2 cups, sifted

ICE CREAM
1 quart	4-6 servings

LEMON
1 medium - juice	2-3 tbs.
1 medium - rind	1/2-1 tbs.

MILK
1 quart	4 cups (American) OR 5 cups (Canadian)
1 pint	2 cups

NUTS
1 lb. almonds (in shell)	1-1/4 cups nutmeats
1 lb. pecans (in shell)	1-1/2 cups nutmeats
1 lb. peanuts (in shell)	2 cups nutmeats
1 lb. walnuts (in shell)	1-3/4 cups nutmeats

ORANGE
1 medium - juice	5-6 tbs.
1 medium - rind	1-2 tbs.

RAISINS
1 lb.	3 cups

SUGAR
1 lb. granulated sugar	2 cups
1 lb. confectioner's sugar	3 1/2 cups, sifted
1 lb. brown sugar	2 1/4 cups, firmly packed
1 lb. powdered sugar	2 1/3 cups

COOKING TERMS & DEFINITIONS

Almondine: Made with shredded, blanched almonds which have been browned in butter.

Appetizer: A small serving of food or beverage served before, or as the first course of a meal.

Au Gratin: With a cheese topping or crust.

Bake: To cook in oven by dry heat.

Barbecue: To roast on a rack over coals or on a spit, usually basting with a sauce.

Baste: To spoon liquid or fat over food while it cooks, to add flavor and prevent drying of the surface.

Batter: A mixture of flour, liquid, etc. which can be beaten or stirred.

Beat: To mix with a brisk, regular motion that lifts mixture over and over, making the mixture smooth and introducing air.

Blanch: To immerse in boiling water, then draining and rinsing with cold water, generally in order to loosen skin or set color.

Blend: To thoroughly mix two or more ingredients.

Boil: To cook in steaming liquid in which the bubbles are breaking on the surface (212 ° F).

Braise: To brown food in a small amount of hot fat, then cooking tightly covered either in the oven or in top of the stove, in a small amount of liquid.

Bread: To coat food in flour, egg and crumbs.

Broil: To cook over or under direct heat.

Broth: Liquid in which meat or poultry has been simmered.

Canape: A tiny piece of bread, or a cracker, which is topped with an appetizer.

Capons: A castrated male chicken, which grows large and has tender meat.

Chill: To allow to become thoroughly cold.

Chop: To cut fine or coarse pieces with a sharp knife.

Coat: To cover with a thin film, e.g. flour, crushed nuts, crumbs, etc.

Compote: Stewed fruit which has been slowly cooked in a sugar syrup to keep its natural shape.

Cool: To let stand at room temperature until no longer warm.

Cream: To work foods until soft and fluffy, ordinarily applied to mixing of sugar and shortening.

Creole: A tomato sauce which is well seasoned and contains celery, onions, green peppers, etc.

Crouton: Cubes of toasted or fried bread used in soups, in garnishes, in salads, etc.

Cube: To cut into pieces with six equal square sides.

Cut In: To combine solid fat with dry ingredients using two knives, pastry blender, etc.

Deep-Fry: To cook food in a deep layer of hot fat.

11

COOKING TERMS & DEFINITIONS

Deviled: Prepared with hot seasonings or spices.

Dice: To cut in very small cubes.

Dissolve: To mix a dry substance with liquid until it is in a solution.

Dot: To scatter bits (e.g. butter) over a food which is to be cooked.

Dough: A mixture of liquid, flour, etc. which is stiff enough to be handled or kneaded.

Dredge: To coat with flour.

Drippings: Fat and juice resulting from cooking meat or poultry.

En Brochette: Cooked on a skewer.

Fillet: Long thin boneless strip of fish or meat.

Flake: To break lightly into small pieces with a fork.

Fold In: To cut down through the center of a batter to the bottom with the edge of a spatula, and to lift from the bottom to the top, repeating until foods are blended.

Frost: To cover with icing.

Fry: To cook in hot fat.

Garnish: To decorate food for eye and taste appeal using contrasting colors of food.

Giblets: The liver, heart and gizzard of poultry.

Glaze: To coat a food with syrup or jelly to give a luster.

Grate: To reduce food to small particles by rubbing against a grater.

Grind: To crush in a food chopper.
Hors d'Oeuvres: A variety of appetizers.

Julienne: Food cut into match-like strips.

Knead: To work dough with a pressing motion, accompanied by folding and stretching.

Leavening: Ingredients which make soda, baking powder, yeast.

Mash: To reduce to a soft pulpy state.

Melt: To liquefy by applying heat.

Meringue: A stiffly beaten mixture of egg whites, sugar and flavoring.

Mince: To cut or chop food into very small pieces (finer than chopping).

Mix: To combine two or more ingredients, usually by stirring .

Mocha: Coffee flavor, or a combination of chocolate and coffee.

Pan-Broil: To cook meat on a hot dry surface, pouring off grease as it accumulates.

Pan-Fry: To cook in a small amount of fat in a skillet.

Parboil: To boil until partially cooked. Cooking is generally completed by another method.

Pare: To cut off outside covering, e . g. carrots, potatoes.

COOKING TERMS & DEFINITIONS

Partially Set: To chill to consistency of unbeaten egg whites.

Peel: Strip off outside covering, e.g. oranges, bananas.

Pit: To remove pits or seeds from fruit.

Poach: To cook in simmering liquid to cover, retaining original shape of food.

Pot-Roast: To cook less tender cuts of meat in a little liquid, with or without browning first.

Preheat: To heat to desired temperature before placing food in oven.

Puree: To press cooked food through a sieve, making it a smooth, thick mixture.

Render: To free fat from connective tissue on low heat until fat melts and can be drained off.

Roast: To cook by dry heat, usually in the oven.

Saute: To cook in a small amount of fat on low heat.

Scald: To heat to temperature just below boiling point.

Sear: To brown surface rapidly at high temperature.

Sift: To pass through a sieve.

Simmer: To cook in liquid at a temperature just below boiling.

Skewer: A long pin of wood or metal on which food is placed and held in shape while cooking.

Skim: To remove film that forms.

Sliver: To cut or shred into long, thin pieces.

Stew: To cook covered in a small amount of simmering or boiling water for a long time.

Stock: The liquid in which meat, poultry, fish or vegetables have been cooked.

Toast: To brown food by the application of direct heat.

Torte: A rich cake, usually made of crumbs, nuts, eggs, etc.

Toss: To lightly mix ingredients without mashing.

Until Set: Until a liquid has become firm.

Whip: To beat rapidly to increase volume by the incorporation of air.

RECOMMENDED FREEZING STORAGE TIMES

MEATS:

Beef...8-12 months
Hamburger (minced meats)...........4- 6 months
Beef or calves liver.............................3-4 months
Lamb...8-12 months
Poultry (whole)................................6-8 months
Broilers & cut-up poultry...............4-6 months
Turkey..6-8 months
Giblets (except liver)........................2-3 months
Poultry livers........................less than 1 month
Veal..6-8 months
Hot Dogs..2-3 months

FRESH VEGETABLES:

Vegetables should be scalded before freezing.
Place in a wire basket and immerse in boiling
water for no more than 4 minutes. Then cool
immediately by plunging vegetables into ice
water. Drain, wrap and freeze immediately.

Asparagus (in 2 inch pieces)..........6- 8 months
Beans, green or wax.......................8-12 months
Broccoli..12 months
Brussel Sprouts..............................8-12 months
Carrots (sliced)....................................12 months
Carrots (small whole).........................12 months
Cauliflower...12 months
Corn on the Cob.............................8-12 months
Peas...12 months
Spinach...12 months

FRUITS:

Raspberries, cranberries, and blueberries
may be frozen without sugar or syrup. Wash
well and pack. Freeze immediately.
Length of freezer storage....................12 months

Strawberries: Wash well, slice if desired.
Sprinkle with sugar (use 1 lb. to approx. 4-5
lbs. berries) and mix gently.
Length of freezer storage...................12 months

Cantaloupe and watermelon: Fruit should be
ripe and firm. Dissolve 1/3 cup sugar and
1/3 cup orange juice in 2 cups boiling water.
Cool to 70 degrees. Pour over fruit which has
been cut into balls or cubes.
Length of freezer storage................6-8 months

Sandwiches: Use butter instead of mayonnaise as a spread. Day-old bread is best.
Fillings containing jelly, salad dressing and
mayonnaise make bread soggy. Ideal fillings:
salmon, tuna, cream cheese, Cheddar cheese,
cooked egg yolks (whites tend to become rubbery), peanut butter.
Length of freezing storage...less than 1 month

Egg yolks or Egg whites: To freeze yolks, add
2 tbs. sugar or 1 tsp. salt to each cup of yolks.
Nothing need be added to the whites. Never
freeze eggs in the shell.
Length of freezer storage..............8-12 months

Cheese: Wrap well in tinfoil. It may crumble
after long storage, but flavor will not change.

Length of freezer storage:
Cheddar and Processed cheese......6-8 months
Cream cheese.......................................2 months
Cottage cheese...2 weeks

Butter (wrap well in foil)................6-8 months
Milk.. 2 weeks
Ice Cream...2- 4 weeks

Cakes:
   Frosted...2 months
   Unfrosted.....................................3-4 months
   Fruit..8-12 months
Pies (baked or unbaked)................2-3 months
Bread and rolls...................................2-3 months
Cookies (baked or unbaked)..............9 months

FREEZING TIPS

Freezer temperature should be no higher than 0 degrees F.

Freeze foods as quickly as possible by placing them directly against the sides of the freezer.

Label foods for easy identification. Write the name of the food, number of servings, and date of freezing. Different colors of freezing tape are a good idea.

Arrange freezer into sections for each food, space permitting.

FREEZER WRAPPINGS:
heavy duty aluminum foil, transparent wrap, plastic bags, freezer paper.

FREEZER CONTAINERS:
plastic ice cream containers empty coffee cans, oven-proof casseroles, jars (leave air space at top to allow for expansion during freezing).

If you are short of freezing containers, line the containers with plastic bag, fill with desired food, and let freeze solid. Then remove plastic bag from container. This method is ideal when using casserole.s as the container, for food may be removed from the plastic bag when needed, and heated in the original container.

When freezing meals, quart containers can hold 4 servings, pint containers, 2 servings.

Use wide-mouth containers for freezing to avoid the necessity of complete defrosting before removal.

To prevent sticking, spread food to be frozen (berries, hamburgers, cookies, etc.) on a cookie sheet and freeze until solid. Then remove to plastic bags and store.

DO NOT RE-FREEZE MEATS, etc. However, once lt has been cooked, you may freeze the food again, as this is not considered refreezing.

Undercook foods which must be heated before serving to avoid a warmed-over taste.

Slice meats before freezing. They will thaw more quickly.

You may cook meat, poultry and fish while still frozen. Increase cooking time.

Never stuff poultry or roasts before freezing.

Do not unwrap meat when thawing.

Thawing of meat and poultry: allow 2 to 2-1/2 hours per pound at room temperature, and 5 to 6 hours per pound in the refrigerator. Coffee retains that fresh-ground taste when stored in the freezer.

FREEZING TIPS

If you need a lot of ice cubes, make the required amount in advance, and store in plastic bags.

Do not freeze celery, lettuce, cucumbers, carrots or raw tomatoes.

Rice hardens when frozen.

To cook frozen vegetables, do not thaw them before cooking to avoid loss of Vitamin C. Cook minimum time in as little water as possible.

Mashed and stuffed potatoes freeze well. However, omit potatoes from stews, soups, etc. that are to be frozen as cooked potatoes become mushy when frozen in liquid.

Cakes which have been frozen, dry out more quickly when thawed than those which are freshly baked.

Cake defrosts in approximately 2 hours at room temperature. Thaw without unwrapping.

The cookie crumb crust of cheese cake becomes soggy when frozen.

To freeze an unbaked fruit pie, do not pierce the top crust to prevent fruit from drying out. For easiest handling, freeze unwrapped just until frozen; then wrap immediately.

To bake a frozen pie, remove from freezer, unwrap, make several slits in top crust and pop into the oven. Allow 15-20 minutes extra baking time.

To freeze a baked fruit pie, first cool it thoroughly at room temperature, then wrap and freeze.

Foods containing macaroni, spaghetti, or rice tastes warmed-over when thawed and re-heated, so add these ingredients when reheating rather than before freezing.

Defrost baked pies at 400 degrees for 10-15 minutes.

MISCELLANEOUS HINTS

To skin a tomato easily, place a fork through the stem end, plunge into boiling water, and then into cold. Break skin from blossom end and peel back.

An easy substitute for one cup of Medium white sauce is 3/4 cup condensed cream of mushroom soup blended with 1/4 cup cold water.

For fancy ice cubes, place red and green maraschino cherries in compartments of ice cube tray. Fill with water and freeze.

To avoid diluting punches and other beverages, make juice cubes. Just pour fruit juice into ice cube trays and freeze.

Store coffee in refrigerator or freezer to keep it fresh longer.

Tomatoes, oranges, lemons, etc. which have been cut may be placed, cut-side down, on a plate and refrigerated.

Shortening should be stored at room temperature, and butter or margarine should be refrigerated.

When frying, cover skillet with a colander. It will prevent fat from spattering, and yet allow food to brown and steam to escape.

Never shake measuring cup when measuring dry ingredients. Spoon lightly into cup (except for brown sugar), then level with a straight-edge knife.

To measure brown sugar, pack it into a measuring cup until it holds its shape. Level.

To keep a bowl from slipping on working surface, place it on a folded wet towel.

Add a little baking soda to the water when cleaning the refrigerator. It will deodorize it.

Place a lump of charcoal in the refrigerator. It will absorb strong odors.

To keep windows defrosted on cold days, rub alcohol or salt water on the outsides, then polish with paper toweling.

When you find a crack in your favorite dish, if it is not too deep, you may be able to make it invisible by boiling it on low heat for about one hour in sweet milk.

If you have a lot of stamps to lick, cut a potato in half and the exposed surface is perfect to moisten them.

DIETING HINTS

Follow the three B's while cooking: Boil, bake or broil.

Trim all visible fat from foods. One tablespoon of fat contains about 100 calories.

Steer clear of fried foods.

Use non-stick pans - they do not require fat for cooking.

Use a low-calorie cooking spray instead of butter or fat when sauteing.

Do not use gravies or cream sauces.

To remove fats from braised foods, soups, etc. refrigerate. The fat which congeals on the surface can then be easily removed.

Eat slowly and chew well.

Sit down when eating. Do not eat while standing or talking on the telephone.

Weigh your-self regularly and often.

Diet silently.

Skim milk and buttermilk contain the same calories - 87 per 8 oz. serving - nearly half the amount in whole milk.

Buy tuna which is packed in spring water rather than oil.

Buy skim milk cheeses.

Substitute dry cottage cheese (pot cheese) for cream cheese in recipes.

Four to five tablespoons sugar equals 1 tsp. liquid sweetener.

Use cornstarch instead of flour to thicken your low-cal sauces.

Canned fruit may be substituted for fresh if all the syrup is drained off and the fruit is washed well under cold water.

18

UNUSUAL WAYS TO USE YOUR MICROWAVE

MAKE YOUR OWN LIQUID SOAP

Shave a bar of soap into 3 cups of water.

Microwave on High for 5-6 minutes, stirring after every 2 minutes.

After the soap cools, put it in your soap dispensers.

GET MORE JUICE FROM YOUR CITRUS FRUIT

Before squeezing it, microwave the fruit on high for 30-45 seconds or until it's warm to the touch. You will get more juice with less effort.

SOFTEN AVOCADOS AND ACORN SQUASH

To make it easier to cut a one-pound squash, microwave it on high for 1-1/2 minutes or until it's warm.

For avocados, that need a little ripening, microwave on high for 1 minute. Cool completely before slicing.

WARM UP BRANDY OR OTHER AFTER-DINNER DRINKS

Put 2 oz. in a snifter and microwave on high for 15 seconds.

PREPARE HOT TOWELS FOR DINNER GUESTS

Fold moist washcloths in a nonmetallic basket or dish and microwave on High for 1-2 minutes, or until they are warm to the touch.

OPEN FRESH OYSTERS AND CLAMS

Clean them, then soak them in cold water for at least 3 hours. Put 6 on a platter, cover with plastic wrap or a lid, then microwave on high for 45 seconds or until shells pop open.

WARM UP HAND LOTION OR BABY OIL

Remove the cap, then microwave the bottle on High for 15-30 seconds or until it feels warm to the touch.

NOTES

2 DRINKS

HOT & COLD

BUBBLING HOLIDAY PUNCH

1 pkg (10 o.z) frozen strawberries, thawed
2 limes thinly sliced
2 cans (6 oz) frozen daiquiri mix
2 cups light rum
3 bottles (4/5 quart) Cold Duck

Ice Ring: Pour water into ring mold to depth of 1 inch. Freeze.

Arrange berries and lime slices around mold. Add enough water to anchor fruit to ice. Freeze.

Fill mold with water. Freeze solid.

To Serve: Combine daiquiri mix and rum. Add ice ring very carefully. Pour in Cold Duck.

Yield: 20 servings (5 oz each).

COFFEE LIQUEUR

Boil and dissolve 6 cups water and 4 lbs sugar. Chill. Set aside.

Boil and dissolve 6 cups water and 1 cup instant Coffee. Chill. Set aside.

Combine all ingredients and add 2 large vanilla beans and 1 bottle (4/5) of Vodka or Brandy.

CHERRY SLUSH

7 cups boiling water
1 cup sugar
2 cups cherry-flavored vodka
2 tea bags
1 can (12 oz) frozen orange juice concentrate

Combine boiling water and sugar. Add tea bags. Let steep 3-5 minutes. Remove tea bags; discard. Cool sugar mixture. Add vodka and orange juice concentrate. Pour into a 13" x 9" x 2" baking pan. Freeze overnight. To serve, use a large spoon to scrape across the surface of the frozen mixture. Spoon slush into chilled sugar-rimmed glasses. To rim glasses with sugar, rub the edge of each glass with water; invert glass into a dish of granulated sugar.

SANGRIA

1 bottle red wine
1 oz. orange liqueur
1 oz. Spanish brandy
1/2 oz. gin
8 oz. carbonated water
Sugar, to taste
Slices of lemons, limes and oranges

PARTY SPICED TEA

Grated rind of 3 lemons and 1 orange
2 tsp. ground cinnamon
1 tsp. ground cloves
3 cups sugar
7 cups water
12 tsp. loose tea (or 10 small tea bags)
1 small (6 oz.) can unsweetened pineapple juice

Tie grated rinds and spices in cheesecloth bag; sew or tie up, then set aside. In medium saucepan, stir sugar and 3 cups of the water until dissolved; add prepared spice bag. Bring to a boil, cover and simmer over low heat for 1 hour. Do not remove spice bag.

Bring remaining 4 cups water to boil in kettle, pour over tea, cover and steep 5 minutes. Strain or remove tea bags.

In large pot, combine tea, sugar mixture and pineapple juice, adding water to measure 1 gallon. Bring to boil; remove from heat immediately. Allow to cool, then store in covered jar, leave spice bag in jar.

Yield: 32 cups. Approximately 21 calories per cup.

GRAPE-CRANBERRY HOLIDAY PUNCH

1 can (12 oz.) Welch's frozen concentrated grape juice, thawed
3/4 cup frozen concentrated cranberry juice cocktail, thawed
2 bottles (1 quart each) lemon-lime soda, chilled
2 cups orange juice
Orange and lime slices
Ice

Combine grape juice concentrate, cranberry juice concentrate and orange juice in large punch bowl. Refrigerate until thoroughly chilled. Just before serving, add ice cubes and pour in soda. Float fruit slices for special garnish.

Yield: 25 servings (1/2 cup each)

CHAMPAGNE PUNCH

Combine:
1 bottle champagne
2 cans Hawaiian Punch
1 sliced orange
Frozen Strawberries
2 bottles Ginger Ale
1/2 can frozen Lemonade
1 quart Lime Sherbert
Ice

CHAMPAGNE PUNCH

2 cups vodka
2 bottles pink champagne
1 quart lime sherbert
1/2 cup apricot brandy
2 bottles ginger ale

Chill all ingredients *before* mixing.
Add fruit slices - *no cherries!*

FESTIVE FRUIT PUNCH

Combine:
4 pkgs presweetened Kool Aid
1 can (46 oz) pineapple juice
1/2 can frozen pineapple chunks
2 cups sugar
2 lemons, sliced
4 quarts water

Add: 1 bottle (32 oz.) ginger ale just before serving.
Add ice to desired taste.

PUNCH

Combine:
2 large bottles ginger ale
2 large bottles pineapple juice
1 pint orange sherbert

SPARKLING PEACHES AND CREAM

Note: Chill the fruit, juice, and mineral water thoroughly before blending.

1 can (16 oz) peach slices, chilled
1/2 cup unsweetened pineapple juice, chilled
1 Tbsp sugar
2/3 cup sparkling mineral or carbonated water
1 egg
4 ice cubes
1 Tbsp lemon juice
1/3 cup light cream
1 tsp vanilla
sliced almonds (optional)

In blender combine *undrained* peaches, pineapple juice, egg, ice cubes, sugar, lemon juice and vanilla. Cover and process until smooth and well blended. Stir in light cream; slowly pour in sparkling water or club soda, stirring with an up-and-down motion. Pour into 4 chilled glasses. Garnish each serving with sliced almonds, if desired.

3 APPETIZERS & PARTY TREATS

HINTS

Corkscrew olive:

Hold pitted olive upright between thumb and index finger, turn counter-clockwise while slicing thin, continuous strip from top to bottom. Nice on open-faced sandwiches.

Gherkin fans:

Cut into thin, parallel slices almost to the end. Spread and press uncut end carefully to hold fan in place.

Make vertical grooves with a fork down length of an unpeeled, long slim cucumber. Cut in thin slices.

Radish roses:

With a sharp knife, cut thin, shallow petals around outside almost to the bottom, and repeat for a second layer of petals. Then make 2 or 3 cuts in the center. Place in cold water overnight to blossom.

Carrot curls:

Slice paper-thin slices lengthwise from carrots. Crisp in ice water to curl.

To slice hard-cooked eggs without breaking the yolk, first dip knife into water.

Cut tops from green peppers and hollow out. Use as containers for dips.

Carefully cut about one inch from top of round pumpernickel or cornbread. Scoop out bread, leaving a wall of about one inch. Use as a container for hot hors d'oeuvres (e.g. meatballs,

chicken livers, etc.). Replace top and keep hot in oven until needed.

Scoop out the center of a small rye bread. Stuff with chopped liver. Chill 4-6 hours. Slice in 1/2-inch rounds.

Stuffed cucumber:

Remove the center from a peeled cucumber. Fill tightly with cream cheese. Chill: then cut into 1/4-inch slices.

Toast cups:

Trim crusts from sliced sandwich bread. Brush with melted butter. Press into muffin cups and toast in a moderate oven. A good substitute for patty shells.

Lox & cream cheese hors d'oeuvres:

Wrap 1 teaspoon cream cheese in each slice of lox. Fasten with a toothpick.

HOT CRAB DIP

1 8 oz. package cream cheese
1 Tablespoon milk
1 6-1/2 oz. can flaked crab-
    meat
2 Tablespoons finely chopped
    onion
1 teaspoon horseradish
1/4 teaspoon salt
2 Tablespoons sherry
1/3 cup toasted almonds

Cream cheese with milk. Add crabmeat and other ingredients. Pat in ovenproof dish and bake for 20 to 30 minutes or until hot. Top with almonds.

Serve from chafing dish with rye crackers or Triscuits.

CRABMEAT SUPREME

Make in microwave using full high power.

2 (8 oz.) pkgs. cream cheese
2 (6 1/2 oz) cans crabmeat,
    drained
1 clove garlic, pressed/
    minced
1/2 cup mayonnaise
2 tsp. Dijon mustard
1/4 cup dry white wine
2 Tbls. powdered sugar
Pinch of salt and pepper

Place unwrapped cheese in 3 qt. casserole. Microwave in high 1-1/2 to 2 minutes, or until cheese has softened. Add remaining ingredients. Mix well. Chill several hours or overnight.

When ready to serve, Microwave on high for 5 to 6 minutes. Stir after 3 minutes. Serve hot as dip with crack-ers, Melba rounds, bread sticks, etc.

EGGS WITH IKRA (CAVIAR)

4 eggs
 2 Tablespoons caviar - red or
    black
2 spring onions, parsley or
    dill
1 lemon
l tomato

Boil eggs for 8 minutes. Rinse under cold water to cool. Remove shells. Cut in half lengthwise. Take out the yoke. Fill the white with caviar. Put on small plate.

Garnish: Cut tomato in quarters. Peel off outer skin of spring onions and chop. Chop parsley or   dill. Surround eggs with tomato, spring onions, parsley and sieved yolk. Serve with may-onnaise or wedges of lemon.

Chilled vodka goes well with this. Serves 4.

EGGS STUFFED WITH SALMON

6 hard cooked eggs
2 Tablespoons sour cream
l/2 Tablespoon prepared
    mustard
1 Tablespoon chopped onion

1 Tablespoon capers (more
    for garnish)
2 Tablespoons chopped
    smoked salmon (more for
    garnish)
Fresh dill for garnish
salt and pepper to taste

Remove and mash yolks with sour cream, mustard, salt, pepper, onion, capers, salmon. Stuff filling into whites. Garnish with salmon bits, dill and capers.

HOLIDAY PARTY MIX

1 cup mayonnaise
8 oz. sour cream
2 Tbsp chopped pimento
8 oz. drained and finely
    chopped water chestnuts
1 tsp beef bouillon
1/2 tsp Worcestershire sauce
1/4 tsp garlic powder
1 Tbsp sliced green onion

In medium bowl, combine all ingredients. Mix well. Cover; chill. Stir before serv-ing with fresh vegetables or potato chips.

GUACAMOLE

Mix together the following ingredients:

1 avocado
2 Tbsp lemon juice
1 tsp salt
1 large tomato - peeled, chopped and drained
1/2 cup mayonnaise
1 tsp grated onion
1/4 tsp liquid red pepper seasoning

SNAPPY CHEESE STICKS

2 sticks pie crust mix
1 cup shredded sharp cheddar cheese
1/8 tsp dry mustard
1 tsp paprika

Preheat oven to 425°.
Prepare pie crust mix according to package directions, thoroughly mixing in the shredded cheese.
Add mustard and paprika until the mixture forms a ball.
Roll dough on lightly floured surface to 12 by 8 inch rectangle. With a knife, cut into sticks 1/2 inch wide and 4 inches long.
Place on ungreased baking sheet. Bake in hot oven for 10-12 minutes.

SOUR CREAM DIP

1 cup (8 oz.) sour cream
1 Tbsp finely minced onion
1 tsp salt (to taste)

2 Tbsp chopped green pepper
1 Tbsp prepared horseradish
l tsp pepper (to taste)

Mix in small bowl; chill. Yield: 1 cup.

QUESADILLA PIE (TEX-MEX)

2 cans (4 oz. each) chopped, drained green chilies
4 cups shredded Cheddar cheese (16 oz.)
2 cups milk
1 cup Bisquick
4 eggs

Heat oven to 425°. Grease pie plate (10 x 1-1/2). Sprinkle chilies and cheese in plate. Beat remaining ingredients until smooth (approximately 1 minute with mixer, or 15 seconds in blender). Pour into plate. Bake 25-30 minutes or until knife comes out clean. Let stand 10 minutes before cutting. Serve with sour cream or guacamole. Serves 6 to 8.

TEX-MEX DIP

3 medium sized ripe avocados
2 cans (10 1/2 oz each) plain or jalapeno-flavored bean dip
3 medium tomatoes, cored, halved, seeded and coarsely chopped (2 cups)
2 cans (3-1/2 oz. each) pitted ripe olives, drained and coarsely chopped
Large round tortilla chips

2 Tbsp lemon juice
1/2 tsp salt
1/4 tsp pepper
8 oz. sour cream
1/2 cup mayonnaise
1 pkg taco seasoning mix
1 pkg shredded cheddar cheese

Peel, pit and mash avocados in a medium-size bowl with lemon juice, salt and pepper. Combine with sour cream, mayonnaise and taco seasoning mix in bowl.
To assemble: Spread bean dip on a large shallow serving platter; top with seasoned avocado mixture; layer with sour cream-taco mixture; Sprinkle with chopped onions, tomatoes and olives; cover with cheddar cheese.
Serve chilled or at room temperature with round tortilla chips on the side.

ZIPPY RAREBIT SPREAD (DIP)

4 oz. grated Cheddar cheese
1 tsp Worcestershire sauce
6 slices bacon, cooked and crumbled
8 oz. cream cheese
Dash of liquid hot pepper

Combine everything except bacon over boiling water or in heavy saucepan over low heat. Cook. Stir frequently until smooth and bubbly. Blend in bacon bits. Pour in crock. May be served hot or cold. Serve with crackers.

THREE CHEESE BALL

8 oz. cream cheese
4 oz. shredded blue cheese
1 Tbsp Worcestershire sauce
4 oz. cheddar cheese
1 Tbsp minced onion
1/2 cup chopped walnuts

Leave cheese at room temperature for approximately 2 hours. Place all ingredients except nuts in a mixing bowl. Mix with mixer until all ingredients are thoroughly combined. Shape into a ball and roll in chopped nuts. Wrap in wax paper and refrigerate until completely chilled.

HANKY PANKIES

(Freezes Well)
1 lb. ground beef
1 tsp red pepper
1/2 onion or garlic salt (can use fresh garlic instead of garlic salt)
2 pkgs. cocktail rye bread
1 lb. ground pork sausage
1/2 tsp oregano
1 lb. Velveeta cheese

Brown both meats and drain well. Add rest of ingredients and stir over warm heat to melt cheese.
Spread mixture on rye bread. Freeze on cookie sheet. Then put each piece in plastic bag to freeze.
When ready to use, broil 4 to 5 minutes.

DEVILED EGGS DELUXE

6 hard boiled eggs
3 Tbsp mayonnaise
2 tsp prepared mustard
2 tsp lemon juice
1-1/4 tsp worcestershire sauce
1/4 tsp salt
1/8 tsp pepper
parsley
paprika

Cut eggs in half lengthwise. Remove yolks. Mash yolks in mixing bowl. Combine yolks with sauce, salt and pepper. Blend well. Refill egg whites. Garnish with parsley, sprinkle with paprika.

GARLIC CHEESE SPREAD

Take a large package of Philadelphia cream cheese. Soften with milk. Add 2 lbs. cottage cheese (optional) and a finely cut or grated onion. Add garlic powder or garlic salt.

QUICHE LORRAINE

1 unbaked 9-inch pastry shell
4 slices bacon
1/4 cut finely chopped onion
1-1/2 cup shredded Swiss cheese
4 eggs, slightly beaten
1-1/3 cup milk
3/4 tsp salt
1/2 tsp dry mustard
1/8 tsp white pepper
1/8 tsp ground nutmeg

Preheat oven to 450° F. Bake pastry shell for 5 minutes; remove from oven. Set oven temperature to 400° F. Fry bacon until crisp; drain and crumble. Cook onion until transparent in small amount of bacon fat; drain. Sprinkle bacon and onion over bottom of pastry shell. Cover with cheese. Blend together eggs, milk and seasonings; pour over cheese. Bake for 10 minutes; reduce heat to 350° F and bake 30-35 minutes longer or until a knife inserted in center comes out clean. Makes 6 to 8 servings.

BLUE CHEESE SPREAD

1 (8 oz) pkg cream cheese
1 (4 oz) pkg blue cheese, crumbled
1/4 tsp garlic powder
2 Tbsp milk
1 Tbsp anchovy paste
Assorted crackers

Let cheese stand at room temperature 15 minutes. Combine cheese with remaining ingredients, except crackers. Serve on crackers. Makes about 1-1/2 cups; refrigerate leftovers.

26

"PHILLY" CHEESE BALL

1 (8 oz) pkg Cracker Barrel brand sharp Cheddar flavor cold pack cheese food
1 (8 oz) pkg Philadelphia cream cheese
2 tsp chopped pimento
2 tsp chopped onion
1/2 tsp lemon juice
2 tsp chopped green pepper
1 tsp Worcestershire sauce

Combine cold pack cheese food and softened cream cheese; mix until well blended. Add remaining ingredients; mix well. Mold into ball shapes, using 2 cold pack containers lined with plastic wrap. Chill until firm. Unmold and garnish with pimento strips, if desired. Yield: 2 balls.

GARLIC-HERB CHEESE SPREAD

1 8 oz. pkg. cream cheese
1/4 stick butter
2 cloves garlic
2 dashes Fine Herbs

In food processor or blender, chop garlic first. Cut up butter and cream cheese and add to garlic. Add herbs. Refrigerate.

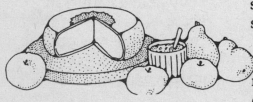

SNAIL-STUFFED MUSHROOM CAPS

2/3 cup softened butter
2-3 cloves garlic, minced
2 tbs. parsley, minced
1 can lg. snails, drained & rinsed
Freshly ground pepper
18 large mushroom caps
2 tsp. green onions, minced
1/2 tsp. salt

Cream butter and stir in garlic, parsley, onions, salt and pepper. Place 1 snail in each cap and spoon 1 tsp. of butter mixture on top of snail. Spoon remaining butter mixture over snails in mushrooms. Let stand covered at room temperature 2-3 hours or refrigerate overnight.

Bake uncovered in a shallow baking dish in preheated 475° oven about 6-7 minutes or until hot and bubbly. Can be served on individual plates or from a chafing dish. Serves 6.

CHEESY STUFFED MUSHROOMS

40 mushrooms
3/4 cup Parmesan cheese
1 8 oz. pkg. softened cream cheese
small amount of milk
slivered almonds

Pull stem out of mushrooms. Combine cream cheese, Parmesan cheese and enough milk to make a thick paste. Fill mushroom caps. Put almond on top.

Broil 3-5 minutes. Serve hot. Yield: 40.

CAVIAR EGG MOLD

18 hard-boiled eggs; separate egg whites and yolks

To grated whites, add:
3/4 cup mayonnaise
2 pimentos, finely chopped, optional
1/2 cup chopped parsley
salt and pepper to taste

To grated yolks, add:
3/4 cup mayonnaise
1 small jar red caviar
pinch of dry mustard
salt and pepper to taste

Oil 9" ring mold. Put egg mixture in mold layers: white, yellow, white. Refrigerate at least 12 hours. Turn out on platter. Serve with party rye, melba toast, or crackers. Serves 12.

CAVIAR PIE

8 hard-boiled eggs
1 stick softened butter
grated fresh onion
12 oz sour cream
1 jar caviar

Grate eggs. Add softened butter, then cream eggs and butter together. Pat into a 9" buttered pie pan. Grate onion over egg/butter mixture. Cover with sour cream. Place in freezer for 1 hour. Remove from freezer and spread caviar on top. Refrigerate until ready to serve. Cut into pie-shaped wedges and serve with melba toast.

MARVELOUS CHEESE SPREAD

8 oz softened cream cheese
1/2-3/4 cup softened butter
1 tsp chopped capers
1 tsp chopped chives
1 tsp chopped parsley
1 tsp Dijon mustard
1 chopped anchovy fillet
1 tsp chopped onion
pinch of salt and pepper
caraway seeds

Blend all ingredients together. Put in 2 crocks and serve.

FARMERS CHOP SUEY DIP

1/2 lg. cucumber
1 green pepper
1 tomato
1 bunch green onions
1 8 oz. pkg. softened cream cheese
1 tbs. dill weed
1/2 cup sour cream
1 tsp. dry mustard
1/2 tsp. salt
1/2 tsp. pepper
1 tsp. Worcestershire sauce

Finely chop all the vegetables. Do not use a blender or a food processor. Combine the cream cheese and sour cream and add remaining seasoning. Fold in the chopped vegetables.

Chill 24 hours. Serve with fresh vegetables.

SUPER DIP FOR VEGETABLES

1 medium onion, chopped
1 8 oz. pkg. softened cream cheese
1 jar Kraft Roka cheese spread
1 jar B-V gravy
2 cups mayonnaise

Put all in blender and mix thoroughly. Should be made a day before serving. Refrigerate. Serves 25.

GUACAMOLE DIP

4 ripe avocados, or 2 pkgs. plain frozen avocado dip, defrosted.
1 8 oz. pkg. softened cream cheese
1/2 jar Picante sauce
1 tsp. lemon juice
1 tsp. garlic salt
onion flakes to taste

Combine all ingredients in blender and blend well. Serve with Doritos. Yield: 1 pint.

Variation: Chopped tomatoes and/or crabmeat may be added after blending.

AVOCADO LOG

1 lg. ripe avocado (1 cup)
1 clove garlic, minced
1/2 tsp. salt
2 oz. grated sharp cheese
1 6 oz. pkg. finely chopped toasted cashew nuts
1 8 oz. pkg. softened cream cheese
2 tsp. lime juice
1/2 tsp. Worcestershire sauce
Dash of Tabasco sauce
paprika

With sterling silver fork, mash avocados. (Use of silver fork prevents discoloration of avocado.) In a bowl combine avocados with remaining ingredients. Cover and chill mixture for about 30 minutes. Take 1/2 of mixture and mold into a log. Then do the same with the remaining 1/2 of mixture. Roll each log in paprika and chill, wrapped in clear plastic wrap for at least 2 hours. Servo with crackers or tortilla chips. Can be mixed in a food processor. Delicious with Margaritas.

Note: if you locate Spanish paprika, it is preferred.

ARTICHOKE DIP

1/2 cup grated Parmesan cheese
1 can of artichoke hearts, cut
1 clove garlic, pressed
1 cup mayonnaise

Combine all ingredients. Chill and serve as a dip. It can also be used as a stuffing for tomatoes and served warm or cold.

ARTICHOKE MOLD

2 15 oz. cans artichokes, finely chopped
6 hard boiled eggs, finely chopped
12-14 small sweet pickles, finely chopped
1 sm. can black olives, pitted
1 oz. black caviar
1 tbs. gelatin
1/4 cup cold water (scant)
1/2-3/4 cup mayonnaise

Sprinkle gelatin over the cold water. Set aside. Combine first 5 ingredients and then add to gelatin mixture. Pour into greased 4 cup mold and chill overnight. Unmold and frost with mayonnaise. Best served on thin sliced bread.

MEXICAN PIZZA DIP

10 inch round serving plate.

Spread in layers in the order given.

1 8 oz. pkg. cream cheese, softened
1 #303 can chili - no beans
8 oz. Mozzarella cheese, shredded
1 1/2 lg. green peppers, finely chopped
1/2 onion, finely chopped

1 small can black olives, sliced

Serve at room temperature with Doritos.

SPINACH DIP

1 pkg. frozen chopped spinach, thawed and drained
1 cup mayonnaise
1 cup sour cream
1 small pkg. Hidden Valley original salad dressing mix

Defrost spinach. Drain thoroughly. Combine with other ingredients. Chill. Serve with crackers. Serves 8 to 12.

PRETTY PINK PARTY DIP

1 8 oz. pkg. Neufchatel cream cheese, softened
6 oz. sour cream
2 pkgs. Lipton's tomato Cup-A-Soup
2 tbs. red horseradish to taste
1 can cocktail shrimp
1/2 cucumber, chopped, salted and drained (optional)

Mix all ingredients. Add more sour cream to thin out if needed. Serve with chips, Fritos or crackers. Serves 8 to 12.

LOX AND CREAM CHEESE SPREAD

2 8 oz. pkgs. cream cheese at room temp.

2 tbs. milk
1/4 cup chopped radishes
1/4 cup cucumber, chopped, seeded and peeled
1/4 cup chopped green onions
8 slices lox, chopped well

Mix cream cheese with milk. Add remaining ingredients. Mix well, wrap in wax paper and refrigerate 24 hours. Serve on little bagels and/or cocktail rye.
Serves 12.

SALMON APPETIZER

1 7-1/2 oz. can salmon
1 8 oz. pkg. softened cream cheese
1 tsp. lemon juice
2 tsp. grated onion
3 tbs. chopped parsley
2 tsp. red horseradish
1 tsp. salt
1/4 tsp. liquid smoke
1/2 cup chopped pecans

Drain and flake salmon. Combine with cream cheese. Mix with rest of ingredients except nuts and parsley. Form into ball. Refrigerate for 1 hour. Roll in nuts and parsley. Serves 8.

SHRIMP PICK-UPS

1/4 cup mayonnaise
1 tsp. Worcestershire sauce
1 tomato, diced and seeded or 6-7 cherry tomatoes, halved
1 lb. shrimp, cooked and peeled

1/4 lb. cream cheese, softened
1 tbs. grated onion

Mix first 4 ingredients. Add
shrimp and tomatoes. Serve
with toothpicks.

GUACAMOLE DIP

1 avocado, peeled, mashed
1/2 cup chopped tomato
1/4 cup mayonnaise
2 tablespoons chopped onion
1/4 tsp. salt
Dash of hot pepper sauce
2 crisply cooked bacon slices,
crumbled

Combine all ingredients
except bacon; mix well. Add
bacon; mix lightly. Serve
with tortilla chips.
Yield: 1-1/2 cups

CREAMY SPINACH DIP

1 10 oz. pkg. frozen chopped
spinach, cooked, well-
drained
1 cup mayonnaise
1 cup sour cream
1/2 cup chopped parsley
1/4 cup chopped green onion
1 teaspoon dill weed
1/2 teaspoon lemon pepper

Combine ingredients; mix
well. Chill. Serve with assorted vegetable dippers.
Yield: 2-1/2 cups.

Variations:
Substitute plain yogurt for

sour cream.
Substitute reduced calorie
salad dressing for mayon-
naise.

HOT SWISS AND ALMOND SPREAD

1-1/2 cups (6 oz.) shredded
Swiss cheese
1 8 oz. pkg. cream cheese,
softened
1/3 cup mayonnaise
2 tablespoons chopped green
onion
1/8 teaspoon ground nutmeg
1/8 teaspoon pepper
1/3 cup sliced toasted
almonds

Combine all ingredients
except almonds, mix well.
Stir in almonds. Spread mixture into 9-inch pie plate.
Bake at 350°, 15 minutes,
stirring after 8 minutes.
Garnish with additional
toasted sliced almonds, if
desired. Serve with crackers
or party rye bread slices.
Yield: 2-1/3 cups

CRABMEAT PARTY PUMPERNICKEL

1 cup (4 oz.) shredded Swiss
cheese
1/3 cup mayonnaise
1 6 oz. can crabmeat, drained,
flaked
1 tablespoon lemon juice
1 teaspoon dill weed
24 party pumpernickel bread
slices, toasted

Combine all ingredients
except toast; mix lightly.
Spread onto toast. Broil until
cheese is melted.
Yield: 2 dozen

MEXICAN PEANUTS

1-1/2 Tbs. lime juice
2 tsp. ground red chile
salt, to taste
1-1/2 Tbs. vegetable oil
1 lb. shelled peanuts

Preheat oven to 275° F. Mix
lime juice, oil and chile and
toss with peanuts. Place nuts
on cookie sheet or shallow
baking tray and roast for 15-
20 minutes until golden.
Sprinkle with salt if desired.
Cool before storing. Makes 3
cups.

CURRIED ALMONDS

3 Tbs. olive oil
1 lb. whole, unblanched
almonds
salt to taste
1 Tbs. curry powder
1/8 tsp. cayenne

Preheat oven to 300° F. Heat
the oil in a heavy skillet. Add
the almonds and sprinkle
with the curry powder and
cayenne. Cook, stirring, until
slightly darkened, about 2-3
minutes. Remove to a cookie
sheet lined with parchment
paper. Bake 10 minutes or
until crisp. Sprinkle with salt
if desired. Cool before storing. Makes 3 cups.

VEGETABLE PIZZA

2 8 oz. pkgs. Pillsbury
  Crescent rolls
2 8 oz. pkgs. cream cheese
2/3 cup mayonnaise
1 tsp. dill
1 Tbs. minced onion

Heat oven to 375°. Separate dough into 4 rectangles. Place on a 15" x 10" pan or a cookie sheet. Seal perforations. Bake 15-18 minutes until golden brown. Cool completely.

Combine cream cheese, mayonnaise, dill and minced onion. Blend until smooth. Spread over cooled crust. Top with chopped mushrooms, tomatoes, olives, green onions, carrots, etc. Cut into appetizer-size pieces. Refrigerate.

Yield: 60 appetizers.

SPICED NUTS

1 egg white
3/4 cup sugar
1-1/2 tsp cinnamon
1/2 tsp nutmeg
1 tsp water
1 tsp salt
1/2 tsp cloves
2 cups whole walnuts or
  pecans

Beat egg white stiff. Combine spices and sugar in second bowl. Pour nuts into beaten egg whites, toss to coat. Then pour nuts into spice mixture. Toss again. Spread on greased cookie sheet, separating nuts. Toast in 275° F oven for 30 minutes. Cool. Separate nuts again if necessary. Store up to 1 month in airtight container.

CHEESE DOLLARS

1/2 lb. grated sharp Cheddar
  cheese
1/2 cup butter, softened
1 cup flower
1/2 tsp. salt

Mix ingredients together. Roll this dough in a long roll. Wrap in waxed paper and refrigerate (keeps indefinitely). Cut into 1/4 inch slices and sprinkle with paprika and grated Parmesan cheese.

Bake in 500° oven for about 8 minutes, watching closely. May be served hot or at room temperature.

Yield: approximately 4 dozen.

CHEEZY CRAB DIP

12 oz. cream cheese, softened
1 cup sour cream
1 cup shredded Cheddar
  cheese
2 Tbs. mayonnaise
1 Tbs. seafood seasoning
1/4 cup shredded Cheddar
  cheese for topping
1 tsp. prepared mustard
1 tsp. Worcestershire sauce
Garlic powder to taste
1 lb. canned crab meat
1 Tbs. lemon juice

Preheat oven to 375°. In a large bowl, mix together all ingredients except crab meat and cheese for topping. Fold in crab meat. Put mixture into a 1-1/2 quart casserole dish coated with non-stick cooking spray. Bake for 20 minutes. Sprinkle top with additional cheese and bake for 5 minutes more. Serve with an assortment of crackers.

Yield: 12 appetizer servings.

GREEN CHILIES AND CHEESE PIE

2 4 oz. cans green chilies
4 beaten eggs
3/4 lb. Monterrey Jack
  cheese, grated

Great 9" pie plate. Line with chilies that have been rinsed and seeded to lie flat. Cover with cheese, then eggs. Bake in preheated oven 1 hour at 300°.

Serve hot - cut in wedges.

MINIATURE MEATBALLS

2 lbs. ground beef
2 tsp. salt
1/4 tsp. pepper
Stuffed olives
Pickled onions
Barbecue sauce (below)

Combine beef, salt and pepper in mixing bowl. Measure 1 Tbs. seasoned beef for each ball. Mold beef around stuffed olive or small pickled onion. Place in shallow baking dish. Bake at 300° for 20 minutes. Serve hot with barbecue sauce. Yield: 80.

Barbecue Sauce:
4 Tbs. shortening
1 cup chopped onion
4 Tbs. vinegar
4 Tbs. brown sugar
1/2 cup lemon juice
6 Tbs. Worcestershire sauce
2 cups water
2 tsp. salt
1/4 tsp. cayenne pepper
2 cups catsup

Heat shortening in skillet. Add onion and brown. Pour off drippings. Add remaining ingredients and cook over low heat, stirring frequently, 25 minutes, or until thickened. Yield: 4 cups.

TORTILLA BITES

1 lb. Velveeta cheese
1 small can chopped black olives
1 small can green chilies, chopped with juice
1 large pkg. cream cheese
Green onions, chopped

Mix Velveeta and cream cheese together with hand mixer until smooth. Add drained olives, chilies and onions. Spread mixture on large flour tortillas. Roll tortillas. Refrigerate for one day. Cut into 1 to 1-1/2 inch pieces.

CHEESY ARTICHOKE HEART APPETIZERS

2 8 oz. refrigerated Pillsbury crescent dinner rolls
3/4 cup (3 oz.) Mozzarella cheese
3/4 cup (3 oz.) grated Parmesan cheese
1/2 cup mayonnaise
1 14 oz. can artichoke hearts, drained, finely chopped
1 4 oz. can chopped green chilies, drained (optional)

Unroll dough into rectangles; press onto bottom and sides of 15 x 10 x 1 inch jelly roll pan to form crust. Bake at 375° for 10 minutes. Combine remaining ingredients; mix well. Spread over crust. Bake at 375° for 15 minutes or until cheese is melted. let stand 5 minutes before serving.
Yield: 3 dozen.

TUNA PATE

8 oz. cream cheese, softened
2 Tbs. snipped parsley
1/2 tsp. hot pepper sauce
2 Tbs. chili sauce
1 tsp. onion
1 12 oz. can tuna

Blend cream cheese, chili sauce, parsley, onion and hot pepper sauce. Gradually stir in tuna. Beat until well blended. Place in a 4 cup mold. Chill overnight. Unmold on serving plate and serve with crackers.

LILLY'S WORLD FAMOUS SPINACH DIP

Knorr Vegetable Soup Version
1 10 oz. pkg. chopped spinach (thawed and squeezed dry)
1-1/2 cups sour cream
1 cup mayonnaise
1 pkg. Knorr vegetable soup mix
8 oz. can water chestnuts, chopped
3 chopped green onions

Blend well. Cover and refrigerate at least two hours.

Lipton Soup Version
2 cups sour cream
1/2 cup mayonnaise
1/2 tsp. lemon juice
1 envelope Lipton Vegetable soup mix
10 oz. pkg. thawed and squeezed dry spinach
1 can water chestnuts, chopped

Combine all the above. Chill for a few hours.
Yield: 3 cups

Note:
Red onion may be substituted for green onion. For less fat and calories, use light sour cream and mayonnaise.

4 SOUPS & GARNISHES

HINTS

To absorb fat from soup, place a lettuce leaf in the pot and see how fast it absorbs the fat. Remove the lettuce leaf as soon as it ha3 done its job.

Refrigerate soup after cooking. The fat will rise to the top and congeal, for easy removal.

If soup is too salty, add a potato. It will absorb the fat.

Freeze soup in compartments of ice cube trays. Remove cubes when solid, and store in a plastic bag. Defrost as many as needed at a time. Perfect for children's lunch.

When freezing soups, always remember to leave room for expansion at the top of the container.

To minimize scum which forms on soup stock, keep the heat low while cooking. Simmer, don't boil.

To add flavor to soup, add a few empty pea pods. Remove them before serving.

Long slow cooking makes a good soup.

Use 1 teaspoon of salt to 1 quart of soup.

Potato Soup: Heat soup. Pour into individual oven-proof bowls.
Sprinkle with grated cheese and brown under broiler.

Corn soup: to one can creamed corn, add an equal amount of milk.

Add: 2 tablespoons of white wine to cream of tomato soup. 1/4 cup sherry to green pea soup. Garnish with croutons. 1/4 cup sherry to cream of celery or mushroom soup. 2 tablespoons sherry to consomme or onion soup. 2 tablespoons white wine to chicken broth.

If you need grated carrots for the soup: leave on about an inch of green tops. These make perfect handles when grating.

If recipe calls for meat or meat bones and you don't have any, make soup without and just add 2 or 3 tablespoons of butter to cooked soup.

Garnishes: croutons, sprigs of parsley, crumbled potato chips, toast fingers, thin slice of lemon or cucumber.

Add 1 pkg. dry onion soup mix & 2-1/2 cups bouillon to roasts.

ITALIAN CHICKEN SOUP WITH TINY MEATBALLS

Broth:
1 whole chicken, 3 to 4 lbs,
   left whole
1 tsp. salt
4 ribs celery, chopped
2 carrots, chopped
3 fresh tomatoes, quartered,
   or 1 16 oz. can
2 medium onions, sliced
3 quarts water

Meatballs:
1/2 lb. ground sirloin
2 Tbs. grated Romano cheese
1 slice bread, soaked in water
   and squeezed dry egg yolks
1 tsp. dried basil
Salt and pepper to taste

Soup:
Chicken broth (about 2
   quarts)
3 cloves garlic, chopped
2 Tbs. minced basil leaves
Salt and pepper to taste
2 Tbs. grated Romano cheese
2 Tbs. olive oil
1 Tbs. butter
1 bag fresh spinach (10 oz. to
   1 lb.), cleaned
1/4 cup fresh lemon juice

Make the broth: Place the rinsed chicken in a pot with the cold water, add salt and bring to a boil. Remove any scum that floats to the top. Add the celery, tomatoes and onions, cover the pot and keep at a low simmer for 1 1/2 hours. Remove chicken and reserve for another use.

Strain the broth. Makes about 2 quarts.

Make the meatballs: Mix together the beef, cheese, bread, egg yolks, basil and salt and pepper thoroughly. shape into small meatballs, about the size of marbles.

Make the meatball soup: Bring the chicken broth to a boil. Add the meatballs and cook at gentle simmer for about 7 minutes, until meatballs are just cooked through. Make a paste by mashing the garlic, basil and salt, then mixing in the cheese, olive oil and butter. Mix the paste into the soup, add the spinach and lemon juice, and cook 5 minutes longer.

Serves 8.

MATZO BALLS

2 eggs, separated
1 pkg. G. Washington bouillon mix
1/2 cup matzo meal

Beat egg whites and yolks separately, then mix together and add G. Washington. Mix in matzo meal. Add 1 Tbs. chicken soup to mixture. Place in refrigerator for at least 1/2 hour.

Boil *large* pot of water. Meanwhile, make small balls. Place on waxed paper. When water is boiling, drop in balls carefully and boil for 20 minutes.

EGG DUMPLINGS

1 cup self-rising flour
1 Tbs. shortening or butter
1 egg

Sift and measure the flour. Cut the butter into the flour. Break the egg into a measuring cup, then add enough water to come up to the 3/4 cup line. Add to the flour and mix lightly with a fork. Drop by tablespoonfuls over boiling meat and broth or into well greased steamer placed over boiling water. Cook 15 to 20 minutes, until dumplings are tender.

STRACCIATELLA

(Chicken egg drop soup with cheese)

4 eggs
4 tsp. fresh parsley, chopped
   very fine
2 pinches of ground nutmeg
4 tsp. grated Parmesan
   cheese
2 quarts of chicken stock
   (recipe below)

Beat eggs just until blended. Mix in cheese, parsley, nutmeg, and salt to ta.ste. Bring stock to boil over high heat and add egg mixture, stirring gently and constantly with whisk. Continue stirring at simmer for 2-3 minutes. Taste for seasoning and serve at once.

Chicken Stock

1 large chicken
2 quarts cold water, add water, if needed to maintain 2 quarts.
2 stalks celery with leaves
2 sliced carrots
1 large onion, quartered
1 Tbs. salt
1/8 tsp. pepper
4 tsp. fresh parsley, chopped

Put chicken with all other ingredients in large pot. Cover and simmer 2-1/2 hours, or until chicken is tender and pulls away from bone, adding water as necessary. Strain. Refrigerate broth overnight. Fat will float to top. Skim and discard *half* fat. Will keep up to one week in refrigerator.

Soup chicken makes good chicken salad.

Serves 10-12.

CREAM OF ARTICHOKE SOUP

2-3 leeks
6 Tbs. (3/4 stick)
2 (10 oz.) pkgs. frozen artichoke hearts, thawed and coarsely chopped
5 cups chicken stock or vegetable soup stock
1 cup whipping cream
1/4 cup freshly grated Parmesan cheese
Salt and pepper to taste

Cut off the root ends of the leeks; cut the leeks in half lengthwise and rinse under cold running water. Chop the white parts coarsely (you should have 2 cups). You may save the green stems for garnish.

Melt the butter in a large heavy pot over medium head. Add the chopped leeks and cook, stirring 3-4 minutes. Add the artichoke hearts and cook another 2 minutes. Add the stock, bring to a simmer and cook, uncovered, until the leeks and artichoke hearts are tender, about 25 minutes.

When the vegetables are tender, remove the soup from the heat and puree it in a food processor, blender, or food mill. Then strain the soup to remove any fibers.

Return the soup to the pot; add the cream and reheat. Gradually stir in the cheese and season to taste with salt and pepper.

You may garnish with the strips of leek greens if you like.

PEA SOUP

1 lb. green split peas, rinsed
1/2 lb. lean smoked bacon
4 leeks (white part only) sliced
1 medium carrot, diced
1 small garlic clove, minced
1/4 tsp. thyme
1 ham bones with some meat
5 medium onions, chopped
2 large celery stalks, chopped
1 cup dry white wine
1/2 tsp. marjoram
Salt and freshly ground pepper

In a large heavy saucepan or flameproof casserole, combine the split peas, ham bone, bacon, onions, leeks, celery, carrot, wine, garlic, marjoram, thyme and 8 cups of water. Bring to a boil; reduce heat to moderately low; cover and simmer, stirring occasionally, until peas are soft, about 2 to 2-1/2 hours.

Remove the bacon and ham bone. As soon as the meat is cool enough to handle, shred or dice any lean meat and add to soup; discard all fat, bones and gristle. Simmer the soup until the peas are very soft, about 10 to 15 minutes longer. Season with salt and pepper to taste.

This soup can be prepared in advance. Let cool to room temperature, then cover and refrigerate for up to 2 days, or freeze for 1 month. Let soup return to room temperature before reheating.

ARTICHOKE BISQUE

1 (9 oz.) pkg. frozen artichoke hearts
2 chicken bouillon cubes
3 Tbs. chopped onions
2 cups clam or canned evaporated milk
Croutons, optional
1/4 cups water
2 Tbs. butter
2 Tbs. flour
1/4 tsp. basil

In saucepan, bring artichoke hearts, water and bouillon to boil. Reduce heat; cover and simmer about 7 minutes or until artichoke hearts are tender. Keep warm.

Meanwhile, melt butter in saucepan over low heat. Add onion and saute 2 minutes, stir occasionally. Add four and basil; sir constantly for about 3 minutes. Gradually add cream or milk to flour mixture. Simmer, stirring constantly, until thickened - about 2 minutes.

Pour artichoke heart and bouillon mixture and cream or milk into electric blender; puree until smooth. Serve immediately. Yield: 3 cups.

COLD WALNUT CREAM SOUP

1 (6 oz.) pkg. walnuts, unsalted
1 green onion, chopped
1/4 cup sour cream
1/4 tsp. white pepper
2 Tbs. fresh lemon juice
Smidgen of curry powder
1 (14 oz.) can chicken broth
1 cup half and half
1/4 tsp. salt
1/4 tsp. hot pepper sauce or
Worcestershire sauce

Garnish:
Coarsely ground walnuts
Hot Hungarian paprika

Reserve a few nuts for garnish. In a blender or food processor, whirl remaining nuts, broth and green onion until very finely chopped. Transfer to a large saucepan and simmer 15 minutes.

Transfer to a large saucepan and simmer 15 minutes. Cool, then add remaining ingredients except garnish. Correct seasoning, adding 1/4 tsp. sugar if desired. Chill. Top each serving with coarsely ground walnuts and paprika.

SOUTHWESTERN CHOWDER

2 Tbs. oil
1/2 lb. smoked turkey, cubed
1 to 2 large onions, chopped
6 cups (about 2-1/2 lbs.) boiling potatoes, cubed
2 cups mild picante sauce
2 quarts water
2-1/2 cups (about five 6 oz.
  cans) tomato paste
1 pkg. (12 oz.) American
  cheese, cubed

In a large pot combine oil, turkey and onions. Cook until onions are soft. Add potatoes, water, tomato paste and picante sauce. Bring mixture to a boil, cover and simmer for about 20 to 30 minutes or until potatoes are tender. Stir in cheese and simmer until cheese melts completely.

Yield: 15 cups or 10 to 12 servings.

CHILLED TOMATO SOUP WITH MINT

2 lbs. fresh, red, ripe tomatoes
1/2 cup finely chopped
  onion

4 whole allspice, crushed
3 cups rich chicken broth
1 Tbs. chopped fresh mint
3 Tbs. butter
1 clove garlic, finely minced
3 Tbs. flour
1/2 cup sour cream
salt and freshly ground
  pepper

Core the tomatoes and cut them into eights.

Melt the butter in a saucepan and add the onion, garlic and allspice. Cook briefly and add the flour, stirring. Add the tomatoes and broth and stir constantly. Add salt and pepper to taste. Bring to a boil and let simmer about 20 minutes. Strain through a food mill. Let cool; chill thoroughly.

Put the soup in a mixing bowl and add the sour cream, stirring with a wire whisk to blend. Before serving add the mint. Garnish with sour cream if desired.

Note: Small cubes of seedless cucumber are also delicious in this soup. If cucumbers are added, the addition of mint is optional.

Yield: 6 to 8 servings.

PAELLA

1 lb. chorizo or hot Italian sausage
3/4 tsp. crushed saffron threads
8 chicken drumsticks (2 lbs.)
1/3 cup extra-virgin olive oil
1 lb. shrimp, shelled and deveined
4 lobster tails, split lengthwise
1 medium onion, chopped
8 garlic cloves, minced
1 medium bell pepper, chopped
3 cups converted rice
3 cups chicken broth
2-1/2 cups clam juice
2 bay leaves
1 pkg. frozen peas, thawed
1/2 tsp. salt
16 littleneck clams, scrubbed
16 small mussels, debearded and scrubbed
2 tsp. ground black pepper
1/4 cup minced parsley
2 lemons, quartered

Prick the chorizo all over with fork. Place in medium skillet with water to cover and bring to a simmer over moderately low heat; simmer for 10 minutes. Drain the chorizo and slice into 1/2 inch rounds.

In a small bowl, steep the saffron in 2 tablespoons of hot water.

Pat the drumsticks dry with paper towels. In a large skillet, heat the olive oil. Add the chicken and sauté over moderately high heat, turning, until browned all over and nearly cooked through, about 20 minutes. Transfer the chicken to a plate. Add the shrimp to the skillet and cook, tossing for 30 seconds; remove with slotted spoon. Add the lobster tails and cook, turning occasionally, until the shells are red and meat is slightly firm, about 6 minutes. Remove with slotted spoon.

Preheat the oven to 350°. Add the onion, garlic and bell pepper to the skillet and cook over moderate heat until softened, about 5 minutes. Stir in the rice and cook, stirring, until translucent, about 4 minutes. Add the chicken stock, claim juice, bay leaves and saffron liquid. Bring to a boil, reduce the heat to low and cook, stirring occasionally, until the rice is tender on the outside, but still chewy in the center, about 17 minutes. Stir in the peas, salt and pepper. Transfer the mixture to a 14-1/2 inch paella pan or a very large oven proof skillet.

Bury the sausage rounds and shrimp in the rice. Place the meaty ends of the chicken legs in the rice to form a large circle around the pan. Push the clams and mussels into the rice, hinges down. Set the lobster tails on top of the rice, flesh side down.

Bake for 30 minutes or until rice is tender, chicken cooked and clams and mussels are open. Remove from oven and cover loosely with foil or clean kitchen towel for 10 minutes. Sprinkle with parsley and garnish with lemon wedges. Serve directly from the pan.

5 SALADS
& DRESSINGS

HINTS

Salad greens should be torn, not cut.

To crisp greens, put paper towels under washed greens, cover with another towel and refrigerate until all moisture is absorbed.

When a small amount of lemon juice is needed, pierce the lemon with a toothpick and squeeze.

To keep peeled and sliced apples from turning brown, cover them with water and a little lemon or lime juice. Drain and pat before using.

When using a peeled avocado or banana, immerse fruit in lemon juice to prevent discoloration.

To remove the white membrane more easily when peeling an orange or grapefruit, soak the unpeeled fruit in hot water for a few minutes.

To crisp celery, soak in ice water with a slice of raw potato for several hours.

Watercress, parsley and mint will keep for three weeks if washed and drained and then placed in an air-tight jar in the refrigerator.

To perk up soggy lettuce, add lemon juice to a bowl of cold water and soak lettuce in refrigerator in water for an hour.

Store fresh bean sprouts and alfalfa sprouts in a tightly covered jar covered with water. Refrigerate.

NOODLE SALAD

Boil accordion noodles for 20 minutes. Cool. Cut up raw onion, 2 hard-boiled eggs, sweet pickles and tuna. Mix with mayonnaise. Take out of refrigerator one hour before serving.

SPINACH SALAD

1 small can bean sprouts
1 small can water chestnuts
8 slices of crisp bacon, crumbled
1 small onion
2 hard boiled eggs

Add these ingredients to crisp, cleaned spinach. Toss.

Dressing
Combine:
1 cup salad oil
1/2 cup wine vinegar
dash of salt
1/3 cup catsup
1/4 cup sugar
freshly ground pepper

AVOCADO SALAD VINAIGRETTE

2 ripe firm avocados
1/3 cup rich olive oil
1 Tbsp Dijon mustard
 freshly ground pepper to
  taste
pinch of sugar
Juice of 1 lemon
3 Tbsp wine vinegar
salt
fresh parsley, chopped

Peel and slice avocados. Arrange on serving plates and sprinkle with lemon juice. Combine remaining ingredients in jar and shake well. Pour this creamy vinaigrette over avocados and serve immediately as a first course.

LAST MINUTE FRUIT SALAD

1 can (16 oz) pear slices, drained
1 can (11 oz) mandarin orange segments, drained
1 cup miniature marshmallows
1/2 cup celery slices
1/2 cup chopped pitted dates
plain or flavored yogurt

Combine all ingredients except yogurt; mix lightly. Top with yogurt. Serves 6.

SPAGHETTI SALAD

(Fun for cookouts!)
1 lb spaghetti, broken and cooked
1/2 cucumber, chopped not peeled
1 bunch radishes, sliced
1 bunch green onions, chopped
1 small green pepper, seeded and chopped
1 small can or jar chopped pimento
1-1/2 tsp salt
3/4 tsp pepper
1 tsp sugar
1/2 tsp celery seed

1/8 tsp ground oregano
4 hard-cooked eggs, chopped

Dressing:
2 cups mayonnaise
4 Tbsp Durkee's dressing
1 Tbsp yellow prepared mustard
3/4 cup sour cream
3/4 cup cream or milk

Blend dressing ingredients well. Combine with rest of ingredients. Mix well and refrigerate. Serves 10-12.
Note: You may have extra dressing. Store in refrigerator.

FRENCH DRESSING

1 cup salad oil
1 tsp dry mustard
1/3 cup vinegar or lemon juice
1 tsp grated onion
1/2 tsp salt
1 tsp Worcestershire sauce
1/2 clove garlic
1/2 tsp paprika

Rub bowl well with garlic. Mix ingredients. Chill. Shake well or beat before serving.

HONEY DRESSING

2 eggs
1/2 cup honey
1/4 cup lemon juice
2 Tbsp frozen orange juice concentrate
1/8 tsp salt
1/2 cup heavy cream, whipped
2 tsp lemon peel

Beat eggs, stir in honey, lemon juice, orange juice and salt. Cook over low heat until thickened. Cool, fold in whipped cream. Serve fresh with fruit. Yield: 2 cups.

CAESAR SALAD

1 garlic clove, crushed
2 lg. heads Romaine lettuce
Freshly ground pepper
1/2 cup grated Parmesan
  cheese
2 eggs, coddled
1/2 cup olive oil
1/2 tsp. salt
3 tbs. lemon juice
2 tsp. Worcestershire sauce
Mashed anchovies

Mix garlic with oil and let stand overnight. Drain and set aside. Clean and trim Romaine. Wash and break into bite sized pieces. Grind on plenty of fresh black pepper. Add salt and 1/2 cup olive oil. Toss well to coat Romaine. Place shelled eggs in center of salad. Add lemon juice and toss until Salad greens are coated with a creamy dressing. Toss with Parmesan cheese and croutons. Serve at once.

To Prepare the Coddled Eggs:
In a small saucepan, heat water to boiling. Add eggs and cook just 1 minute. Remove eggs and cool under cold running water.

Garlic Croutons
5 slices or 2 cups of stale white or French bread, cut into cubes.
3 tbs. olive oil or salad oil
2 garlic cloves, crushed

Trim crusts from bread. Cut into 1/2 inch cubes. In large skillet, brown garlic in oil over medium heat. Add bread cubes and toss until light brown. Stir occasionally. Remove with slotted spoon. Cool.

TORTELLINI PESTO SALAD

1 cup mayonnaise
1/4 cup (l oz.) grated
  Parmesan cheese
1/4 cup chopped parsley
2 garlic cloves, minced
2 tablespoons milk
1-1/2 tsp. dried basil leaves,
  crushed
2 cups cheese or meat tortellini, cooked, drained
1 cup 2 inch julienne-cut
  carrots
1 cup cherry tomato halves
l/2 cup walnuts, toasted

Combine mayonnaise, parmesan cheese, parsley, garlic, milk, and basil: mix well. Add all remaining ingredients except walnuts: mix lightly. Chill. Stir in walnuts just before serving. Serves 4.

Variation: Substitute 2 cups spiral noodles, cooked for tortellini.

PASTA SALAD MEDLEY

1/2 cup Zesty Italian
  Dressing
1 cup (4 oz.) corkscrew noodles, cooked, drained
1 cup mushroom slices
1/2 cup cherry tomato halves
1/4 cup chopped red or
  green pepper
2 tablespoons green onion
  slices
1/2 cup mayonnaise
1/3 cup (1 1/2 oz.) Grated
  Parmesan Cheese

Pour dressing over combined noodles and vegetables. Cover: marinate in refrigerator several hours. Drain. Combine mayonnaise and cheese: mix well. Add to vegetable mixture; mix lightly. Chill. Makes 4 servings.

ITALIAN PASTA SALAD

1/2 cup mayonnaise
1/4 cup chopped parsley
2 tablespoons milk
1 cup salami or ham strips
1 cup carrot slices
1/4 cup pitted ripe olive
  slices
1/4 cup (1 oz.) grated
  Parmesan cheese
3 oz. spaghetti, broken into thirds, cooked and drained

Combine mayonnaise, cheese, parsley and milk, mix well. Add remaining ingredients; toss lightly. Chill several hours or overnight. Add additional mayonnaise just before serving, if desired. Makes 4-6 servings.

FRUITY CHICKEN SALAD

1/2 cup mayonnaise
1/4 tsp. ground ginger
2 cups chopped, cooked chicken
1-1/2 cups strawberry halves
1 cup celery slices
1/4 cup toasted chopped walnuts
3/4 tsp. salt
Dash of pepper
2 cups pineapple chunks
1 cup seedless green grapes
Lettuce

Combine mayonnaise, salt, ginger, and pepper; mix well. Add chicken, fruit and celery; mix lightly. Chill. Serve on lettuce-covered platter; top with walnuts. Serves 6-8.

Variations:
Serve salad in pineapple shells or on individual salad plates.

Omit walnuts. Substitute chopped apples for strawberry halves and red grapes for green grapes.

Substitute 20 oz. can pineapple chunks, drained, for fresh pineapple; add to chicken mixture just before serving.

VEGETABLE AND CHEESE SALAD

1 cup mayonnaise
1/4 cup chopped parsley
1 teaspoon dried basil leaves, crushed
1 garlic clove, minced
1 8 oz. pkg. Mild Cheddar Cheese, cubed
2 cups broccoli flowerets, cooked
1 cup (4 oz.) natural or tri-color corkscrew noodles, cooked, drained
2 medium tomatoes, cut into thin wedges

Combine mayonnaise, parsley, basil and garlic; mix well. Add cheese, broccoli and noodles, mix lightly. Chill. Arrange tomatoes on serving platter; top with vegetable mixture. Serves 4-6.

INSALATA VERTI ALLA SICILY

1 large head iceberg lettuce, washed, drained, chilled
2 cans (2-1/4 oz.) sliced ripe olives
2 oranges, peeled and white membrane removed - thinly sliced crosswise, or use 1 large can of mandarin oranges
1/4 cup olive oil
1/4 cup orange juice
2 tsp. vinegar
1 tsp. salt
1/4 tsp. paprika

Break lettuce into bit-sized pieces and place in salad bowl. Top with olives and oranges.
Blend other ingredients. Pour over salad.
Serves 10 to 12.

ZESTY SALAD TOSS

2 cups fresh Italian bread cubes
1 bottle (8 oz.) Italian dressing
1 quart torn assorted greens
3/4 cup carrot slices
1 cup green pepper strips
1 cup red onion rings
1 cup tomato wedges

Toss bread cubes with 1/4 cup dressing; placed on cookie sheet. Bake at 350° for 15 to 20 minutes or until golden brown, stirring occasionally.
Pour remaining dressing over green pepper, onion, tomato and carrot. Cover; marinate in refrigerator several hours or overnight. Drain, reserving marinade. Combine bread cubes, vegetable mixture and greens; toss lightly. Serve with marinade.
Serves 6 to 8.

FROZEN FRUIT SALAD

1 1-lb. can cherry pie filling
1 can sweetened condensed milk

1 20-oz. can crushed pineapple, crushed 1 cup nuts, chopped
1 13-1/2 oz. container of Cool Whip

Mix together and pour into an oiled 9-1/2 x 5-1/2 inch loaf pan. Cover with foil and freeze until ready to serve. Slice and serve on lettuce leaves. Serves 12.

HEAVENLY STRAWBERRY MOLD

1 6 oz. pkg. strawberry Jello
1 cup boiling water
1 cup chopped pecans
3 medium bananas, mashed (about 1 cup)
2 10 oz. pkgs. frozen strawberries, thawed and drained
1 20 oz. can crushed pineapple, drained
2 cups sour cream

In medium bowl, combine Jello and boiling water. Stir with rubber spatula until dissolved. Cool. Add bananas, nuts, strawberries and pineapple to jello. Stir. Divide in half.

Pour half of Jello into a 12 x 8 pan. Refrigerate until set, about 1 hour. Keep remaining jello at room temperature. Spread sour cream over set Jello. Pour on remaining Jello. Cover and refrigerate until set.

Serves 8-10.

CHINESE CHICKEN SALAD

2 whole chicken breasts

Marinade:
1/4 cup soy sauce
1 tsp sugar
1 clove garlic, mashed
1 Tbs. dry sherry
1 tsp. hoisin sauce

Bake chicken in marinade until done in 350° oven. Cool chicken. May be cooked day before. Shred when cold.

Salad Ingredients:
1 small head lettuce, shredded
1/2 cup chopped green onions
Fried rice sticks (available in oriental markets - follow package directions)
1/4 cup chopped peanuts
1 tsp. toasted sesame seeds
1/2 cup Chinese parsley, optional

Dressing:
2 tsp. hot mustard
1 tsp. Hoisin sauce
1/2 tsp. salt
1/2 tsp. sugar
1 Tbs. sesame oil
2 Tbs. red wine vinegar
1 Tbs. oil

Mix dressing ingredients well. Toss salad ingredients and chicken with the dressing.

Serves 6.

Note: Hoisin sauce and fried rice sticks available at Chinese specialties stores.

CRAB SALAD

2 lbs. crab meat
4 Tbs. finely chopped chives
6 drops Tabasco sauce
3 Tbs. capers, drained and rinsed if brine-packed
1 tsp. salt
1 cup sour cream
2 to 3 Tbs. dill, as garnish

Clean crab carefully to remove shell and filament fragments. Combine all ingredients except dill; mix gently. Garnish with dill. Salad may be made several hours in advance. Keep chilled until served.

BROCCOLI SALAD

In large bowl, combined 3/4 cup sliced fresh mushrooms and one small red onion.

Add a 10 oz. pkg. frozen broccoli spears, thawed, well-drained, and halved crosswise.

Combine 1/3 cup bottled oil and vinegar dressing and 1/4 tsp. Dijon mustard. Pour over vegetables and toss to coat.

42

6 MEATS

ENTREES

HINTS

Approximate number of days to store meat in refrigerator:

Roast ....2 to 3 days
Ground Meat ....1 to 2 days
Smoked Meat..6 to 7 days
Cooked Meats...3 to 4 days
Steaks and Chops...2 to 3 days
Liver ....1 day
Wieners..2 to 3 days
Leftover Casseroles and Stews ....2 to 3 days

When making a meatloaf, line casserole with foil, leaving enough extending so you can grasp it. Loaf will come out nice and easy.

When freezing stew, leave out the potatoes. They become mushy when frozen in liquid.

When freezing meats and poultry, to prevent sticking when freezing hamburgers, steaks, chicken, etc., place them on a cookie sheet and let them freeze completely. Then remove them to a plastic bag.

STEAK AU POIVRE

2 6 oz. steaks (tenderloin, strip, rib eye, skirt)
1 Tbs. cracked black pepper
1 Tbs. butter
1 Tbs. oil
2 Tbs. cognac (brandy)
4 Tbs. creme fraiche or heavy cream

Cover the steak with the cracked pepper and press it into the meat with the palm of your hand. Melt the butter and oil in a heavy-bottomed frying pan. Raise the heat and brown the steaks on each side. Lower the heat and cook until done. For rare meat, about 3 minutes on each side is sufficient. For well-done, cook about 5 minutes on each side. Remove the steak to a warm serving dish and cover with foil to keep warm.

Pour off the fat and add the cognac to the pan, scraping up the brown bits as it cooks. Add the creme fraiche and mix well. Taste for salt and add as necessary.

Place the steaks on individual plates and spoon the sauce over them.
Serves 2.

POT ROAST SUPREME

1 Tbs. flour
1/2 tsp. pepper
1/2 tsp. onion powder
3 lbs. bottom round rump roast
1 large onion, quartered
1 bay leaf
8 potatoes, quartered
1 tsp. salt
1/2 tsp. garlic powder
1/2 cup oil
1 clove garlic
2 cups boiling water
1 lb. carrots, halved

Mix flour, salt, pepper, garlic powder and onion powder in shallow dish. Dredge meat in mixture. Cover bottom of dutch oven with oil and heat. Add meat, onion and garlic, then brown. Add boiling water, bay leaf and carrots. Simmer for 2-1/2 hours.

Add potatoes and simmer for 1-1/2 hours or until meat and vegetables are tender.

FAJITAS

1 lb. beef skirt steak
1 tsp. cumin
1/3 cup Worcestershire sauce
1 tsp. liquid smoke
1/2 medium yellow onion, sliced into rings
1 clove garlic, chopped
1 Tbs. chopped fresh cilantro
1/4 cup soy sauce
Juice from 1 lemon
Pepper to taste

Trim fat from skirt steak; pound lightly to tenderize. Place in long non-metallic pan. Combine remaining ingredients; pour over meat. Cover and refrigerate overnight.

Drain marinade, reserving meat and onion rings. Place onion rings in foil and cook on grill while meat is grilling over hot coals. When meat and onions are done, remove from grill; cut meat into strips. Serve with warm flour tortillas, with guacamole, pico de gallo, sour cream and grated cheese.

Yield: 4 servings.

LAMB PAPRIKASH

2 Tbs. sunflower oil
1 cup sliced green pepper
3 lbs. lamb, from leg, cubed
Salt to taste
1/2 cup flour
1-1/4 cup sour cream
1/2 cup onion, chopped
2-1/2 tsp. paprika
1 med. tomato, chopped
2 cups water
Parsley

Heat oil in large pot, add onions and cook until translucent. Add peppers, paprika and lamb and cook until browned. Add tomato and salt. Add water and let simmer for 30 minutes. Add flour to thicken. If desired, serve over potatoes. Garnish with sour cream and parsley.

SCOTCH LAMB

1 leg of lamb
2 talks of celery
2 to 3 cloves garlic
1 onion, chopped
1 stalk celery, chopped
Salt and pepper
2 carrots
2 turnips
1 to 2 cups water or stock

1 carrot, chopped
2 to 3 Tbs. oil

Bone the leg of lamb without cutting the meat open. Cut the carrots, celery and turnips into small strips. Sliver the garlic. With a sharp knife, make a hole in the lamb and insert one of the vegetable strips. Continue until all the vegetables and the garlic have been used. Season with salt and pepper.

Brown the lamb in the oil and place in the oven. After 45 minutes, add the chopped onion, carrot and celery. Continue roasting until the lamb is done. This should take another 45 minutes. Remove the meat and keep warm. Add some of the water or stock and deglaze the pan a few times to make a sauce.

Slice the lamb onto a serving plate. Pour on some of the sauce and serve hot.

Yield: 8 servings.

BRISKET

Take one whole brisket and cover with raw onion slices. Add roux (mixture of Kitchen Bouquet, flour and water). Then add enough water to cover about 1 inch. Cover with foil and bake 4-5 hours at 275°.

MEAT LOAF

1 can Golden Mushroom
  soup

1/2 cup fine dry bread
  crumbs
1 egg, slightly beaten
1/3 cup water
2 lbs. ground beef
1/2 cup finely chopped
  onions
1 tsp. salt

Mix thoroughly cup of soup, beef, bread crumbs, onion, egg and salt. Shape *firmly* in loaf (8 x 10). Place in shallow baking pan. Bake at 350° approximately 1 hour. Blend remaining soup, water and 2-3 Tbs. drippings. Heat, stirring occasionally. Then pour over meat loaf and bake another 10 minutes.

SAUTEED LIVER WITH SHALLOT VINEGAR

1/4 cup finely chopped shallots
3 Tbs. flour
1 Tbs. vegetable oil
3 Tbs. butter
1/3 cup red wine vinegar
1/4 tsp. pepper
1 tsp. salt
1 lb. calf liver, thinly sliced
  and trimmed

In small saucepan, simmer shallots and vinegar for 5 minutes over low heat; set aside. On plate or wax paper, combine flour, salt and pepper. Cut liver into 3 inch squares and coat in flour mixture, shaking to remove excess.

In heavy skillet, heat 2 Tbs.

butter and oil until butter is melted. Add liver a few pieces at a time and saute over medium heat about 2-3 minutes on each side. Remove liver to serving plate. Stir shallot mixture into skillet and heat gently, scraping up brown bits. Turn off heat and swirl remaining butter. Pour over liver.

Serves 4.

GLAZED BAKED HAM

1 whole 12-14 lb. fully
  cooked, smoked ham, bone
  in
2 cups firmly packed brown
  sugar
8 whole cloves
water
parsley for garnish

Preheat oven to 375°. Place ham, fat side down in deep roasting pan. Add cloves and brown sugar to roasting pan. Pour in enough water to cover 1/3 of the ham. Bake uncovered on lowest rack position for 1-1/3 hours. Turn ham over. Carefully cut off skin and score fat into diamond shapes. Bake 1-1/2 hours longer. Baste occasionally.

Serve hot or cold.

PIQUANT HAM LOAF

Glaze:
1 can (8 oz.) pineapple slices
   in own juice
1 Tbs. cider vinegar
2 Tbs. brown sugar
2 tsp. prepared mustard
2 tsp. cornstarch

Loaf:
2 eggs
1/2 cup fresh bread crumbs
1/4 cup finely chopped onion
6 cups ground cooked ham
1 cup milk
1 tsp. dry mustard
1 lb. ground raw pork
2 Tbs. white horseradish

Glaze:
Drain pineapple and reserve juice. In small saucepan, combine all ingredients except pineapple slices. Cook over medium high heat, stirring until it comes to a boil. Reduce heat and simmer 2 minutes; set aside.

Loaf:
Preheat oven to 350°. Line 9 x 5 x 3 inch loaf pan with foil, letting ends extend over edge of pan. In large bowl combine all ingredients and mix well. Spoon into pan and bake 30 minutes. Remove from oven and arrange pineapple slices on a top, spoon glaze on top and return to oven. Bake 30 minutes more. Cool 5-10 minutes. Pour off excess liquid. Lift loaf from pan. Discard foil. Transfer to serving platter.

THYME-SAUTEED PORK CHOPS WITH APPLE SLICES

1/2 cup flour
8 (1/2 inch thick) loin pork
   chops
4 Tbs. olive oil
Granny Smith or McIntosh
   apples, unpeeled, cut in 1/4
   inch slices
Salt and pepper to taste
4 Tbs. sweet butter
16 sprigs fresh thyme or 2
   Tbs. dried thyme

Combine flour with salt and pepper. Lightly dredge the pork chops in the mixture. Heat half the butter and half the oil in a large skillet. Saute half the chops for 5 minutes on each side. While the chops are cooking, put some thyme under each chop so the herb will stick to the meat. Remove the chops and keep warm.

Add the remaining oil and butter to the skillet and cook the rest of the chops the same way. Remove them and keep warm.

Using the same skillet, saute the apples for 2 to 4 minutes, or until soft, but not mushy. Arrange the chops and apples on a serving dish.

Yield: 5 servings.

SWEET AND SOUR PORK CREPES

8 crepes

1/2 lb. boneless pork shoulder, cubed
Vegetable oil
1 Tbs. red currant jelly
1 (8 oz.) can pineapple tidbits
   in syrup
1 Tbs. brown sugar
1 Tbs. vinegar
1 Tbs. cornstarch
2/3 cup tomato juice
Salt and pepper
Bean sprouts (optional)

Make sure crepes are kept warm while preparing filling.

Heat oil in medium-size saucepan over low heat. Add pork and cook until tender and cooked through, about 10 minutes.

Drain pineapple juice into small saucepan. Add jelly, brown sugar, vinegar and cornstarch and mix well. Add tomato juice and bring to a boil, stirring constantly. Reduce heat and simmer, stirring occasionally, until sauce is thick. Stir in pork and pineapple. Season with salt and pepper.

Preheat oven to 375°. Divide pork mixture between crepes. Roll up and arrange in single layer in shallow heat-proof dish. Cover with foil. Bake 20 minutes. Garnish with bean sprouts if desired. Serve.

SLOPPY JOES

In large skillet, brown 1 lb. ground beef and a chopped onion. Pour off drippings.

Add 1 bottle (8 oz.) of taco sauce, 1 can (4 oz.) drained

chopped green chilies and 1/4 tsp. salt. Simmer 8-10 minutes.

For each serving, spoon mixture over 1/2 cup crushed corn chips and top with grated Cheddar cheese.

PIZZA CASSEROLE

In a 2 quart flameproof casserole, brown 1 lb. ground beef. Pour off drippings.

Add 1/4 lb. sliced mushrooms to casserole. Cook about 10 minutes. Stir in a 12 to 14 oz. jar of pizza sauce.

Top with 1 cup croutons and 1 cup shredded mozzarella cheese. Bake in a preheated 400° oven for 10 minutes.

EASY DOES IT DINNER

1 pkg. (7-1/4 oz.) macaroni and cheese dinner
1 can (16 oz.) tomatoes, cut up
2 Tbs. sweet pickle relish
1/4 cup finely chopped onion
1/2 lb. frankfurters, diagonally sliced
1 Tbs. prepared mustard

Prepare dinner as directed on package, except omitting milk and reducing margarine to 2 Tbs. Add remaining ingredients; mix lightly. Heat thoroughly, stirring occasionally.

Serves 4.

LOW CALORIE BEEF AND POTATO CASSEROLE

4 medium potatoes, diced 1/2 inch
1 lb. ground chuck
1 can (16 oz.) tomatoes
3/4 tsp. oregano
salt
pepper

Grease a 2 quart casserole. Arrange diced potatoes in bottom and sprinkle with 1/4 tsp. crumbled oregano, 1/4 tsp. salt, and some freshly ground pepper. Crumble ground check over potatoes in an even layer and sprinkle with 1/4 tsp. more oregano, 1/4 tsp. salt, and some more freshly ground pepper.

Place canned tomatoes in a bowl and break up with a fork into fairly uniform 1 inch pieces. Spoon these over meat and sprinkle with 1/4 tsp. more oregano, salt and pepper.

Cover and bake in a preheated 400° oven for 40 minutes or until meat is browned and potatoes tender.

Serves 4.

ENCHILADAS

These are delicious and easy! Made in microwave.

Buy tortilla shells - canned or frozen. Fry. Drain on towels. Five shells needed per serving.

Brown hamburger until done.

Chop several onions.

Layer: 1 shell, meat, onions, Velveeta cheese. Cover with hot enchilada sauce.

Repeat 4 times.

Use microwave - cook on high for 5 minutes and serve.

CHICKEN FRIED STEAK

1-1/2 lbs. round steak cut into 1/2 inch pieces
1/2 tsp. pepper
1/2 cup vegetable oil
1/4 cup milk
1 tsp. salt
3/4 cup flour
1 egg

Combine flour, salt and pepper on sheet of wax paper.

Pound steaks until 1/4 inch thick. Dip in flour, then pound as much flour into each steak as possible.

Beat egg and milk in a shallow dish. Dip pounded slices first into egg and milk mixture, then into remainder of flour mixture.

Brown slices in hot oil in large skillet on one side. Turn; cover skillet; lower heat. Cook until meat is tender, about 30 minutes.

PEPPER STEAK

1 lb. round steak

1 tsp. freshly ground pepper
1 medium onion, chopped
2 green peppers, diced
1 cup canned tomatoes,
  drained
2 tsp. soy sauce
1 tsp. salt
2 Tbs. oil
1 garlic clove, minced
1 cup beef bouillon
1-1/2 Tbs. cornstarch
1/4 cup water

Cut the steak into slices 1/8 inch thick. Sprinkle with salt and pepper.

In large skillet, heat oil and add steak, onion and garlic. Cook until meat is browned on all sides.

Add green peppers and bouillon. Cover to simmer for 10 minutes. Add tomatoes and simmer 5 more minutes.

Mix the cornstarch, soy sauce and water. Simmer until meat is soft.

SWEET AND SOUR LAMB RIBLETS

4 lbs. lam riblets
1/2 cup soy sauce
1/3 cup brown sugar
1 Tbs. cornstarch
1/4 cup vinegar
1/2 cup water
2 Tbs. catsup
1/4 cup candied ginger

Remove extra fat from riblets and arrange in shallow roasting pan. Brown riblets in 400° oven approximately 30 minutes. Turn from time to time, pouring off accumulat-

ed fat. When ribs are brown, pour sauce over top of meat and cover pan with foil. Bake in 325° oven for 1-1/2 hours. Turn riblets from time to time, spooning sauce over top. Add water if sauce becomes too thick.

SHORT RIBS

6 or 7 lbs. short ribs
3 Tbs. cider vinegar
6 squirts Teriyaki sauce
2 Tbs. peach marmalade
2 bottles Good Seasons
  Barbecue Sauce
2 cans (29 oz.) peach juice
  (about 1-1/2 cups)
1/2 cup brown sugar
1 Tbs. honey
3/4 cup catsup
2 Tbs. (heaping) duck sauce

Mix all ingredients together. Cook for 2 hours on medium low heat. Use for sauce on ribs.

QUICHE LORRAINE

Pie Dough:
6 oz. flour
1/4 cup water
4 oz. shortening
dash of salt

Mix together and roll the enough. Line pie tin with dough. Bake at 350° for about 15 minutes - not brown.

Quiche Filling:
3 oz. diced Swiss cheese
3 tsp. diced onions
3 oz. diced ham

4 eggs
1 cup milk
4 strips bacon

Saute bacon and onions first until light in color. Pour this mixture in baked pie pan.

Add ham and cheese. Mix eggs with milk and seasoning and add on top of ham and cheese in pie pan.

Bake 25 minutes at 350°.

FAST STIR-FRY

1 lb. cube steak
1 clove garlic, crushed
1/2 cup white wine
1 tsp. Worcestershire sauce
2 Tbs. oil
1 medium onion
1 Tbs. cornstarch
1/2 tsp. salt
1/4 tsp. pepper

Slice cube steak into thin strips. Brown in oil with garlic over medium-high heat. Remove meat. Slice onion; stir-fry 1 minutes. Add mixture of white wine, cornstarch, Worcestershire sauce, salt and pepper. Return beef to skillet. Heat through.

CHILI

2 lbs. flank steak, cut into 1/2 inch pieces
2 lbs. coarsely ground flank steak
2 lbs. boneless pork shoulder, coarsely chopped

1 tsp. fresh oregano or 1/2 tsp. leaf oregano, crumbled
4 can s (7 oz. each) chili salsa or 4 cans (8 oz. each) hot taco sauce
1 Tbs. *each* mild, medium and hot New Mexico chili powders, or 1 to 3 Tbs. chili powder
Salt
1/4 cup vegetable oil
1 tsp. ground cumin
1/2 cup chopped celery
2 cloves garlic, minced
4 medium tomatoes, skinned and chopped, or 1 can (10 oz.) whole tomatoes, drained
3 medium onions, finely chopped (1-1/2 cups)
4 Anaheim chilies, roasted, peeled and chopped, or 1 can (4 oz.) chopped green chilies

Brown cup-up and ground flank steak in 2 Tbs. of oil in kettle; lower heat; cover. Simmer, stirring occasionally for 45 minutes.

Brown chopped pork in remaining 2 Tbs. oil in large saucepan; lower heat; cover. Simmer, stirring occasionally for 45 minutes. Remove pork with slotted spoon; add to beef. Pour pan juices into 2 cup glass measure; let fat rise to top. Skim off 4 Tbs. of the fat and return to large saucepan. Add remainder of pan liquid in glass measure to meat mixture; add cumin and oregano; simmer 30 minutes. Add chili powders, chilies and garlic; cover; simmer 30 minutes.

Saute onion and celery in the 4 Tbs. fat in saucepan, about 5 minutes. Add tomatoes and chili salsa; lower heat, cover; simmer 30 minutes. Add chili powders, chilies and garlic; cover; simmer 30 minutes.

Add salsa mixture to meats. Cook over medium heat for 1 to 1-1/2 hours, stirring frequently. Lower heat and simmer the last 30 minutes of cooking, stirring every 10 minutes to prevent sticking. Taste, add salt if needed.

VEAL SCALOPPINI, BOLOGNA STYLE

2 lbs. veal scaloppini
2-1/2 Tbs. olive oil
2-1/2 to 4 Tbs. Marsala wine, dry white wine
12 slices Gruyere or Emmenthal, or 5 Tbs. grated Parmesan cheese
Flour
3 Tbs. butter
Salt and pepper
12 slices raw Parma ham

Lightly flatten veal; dip slices in flour. Heat oil and butter in a large heavy frying pan; saute veal quickly on both sides until tender and golden brown. Transfer to a baking pan. Season with salt and pepper.

Preheat oven to 425°. Add wine to fat remaining in the pan; cook for a minute or so until slightly reduced, stirring the crusty bits from the bottom with a wooden spoon. Pour this mixture over the veal, place a slice of ham and one of cheese (or sprinkle the ham with a generous teaspoon of Parmesan cheese). Put into a hot oven just long enough to melt the cheese.

Yield: 6 servings.

SAUTEED BREADED VEAL CHOPS

3 veal rib chops, divided into 6 chops and pounded flat
2 eggs, lightly beaten with 1 tsp. salt, in a soup plate
1-1/2 cups fine, dry unflavored bread crumbs, spread on a dish
6 Tbs. butter

Dip each chop in beaten eggs, coating both sides and letting excess egg flow back into the plate. Dredge the chops in crumbs, pressing crumbs in with your hands.

Choose a skillet that can hold the chops in a single layer. Put in the butter and melt it over medium-low heat. When the butter foam subsides, slip the chops into the skillet. Cook for 3 minutes on 1 side, until a dark golden crust has formed, then turn and cook 3 minutes on the other side, watching the butter to make sure it does not burn. When done, transfer the chops to a warm platter and serve immediately.

Yield: 6 servings.

7 POULTRY

ENTREES

HINTS

Rub poultry with lemon juice before cleaning. This will eliminate odor.

Always stuff turkey loosely if you don't want it to burst. Use one cup of stuffing for every pound of turkey.

For a nicely browned turkey, rub with a mixture of 1 Tbs. paprika and 3/4 cup butter.

Always season cavity of poultry, as well as the skin.

If you are freezing leftover stuffed turkey, remove stuffing immediately after the meal is over, to avoid food poisoning.

Covering a turkey with a tent of foil will prevent it from becoming too brown.

Cut cranberry sauce into thick slices and cut with a small cookie cutter. This makes a lovely garnish.

DEEP-FRIED PECAN CHICKEN WITH GINGERED PLUM SAUCE

4 boneless chicken breast
   halves
1 tbs. Dijon mustard
1/4 tsp. black pepper
2 egg whites, room temperature
Vegetable oil
1 tbs. sherry
1 tsp. salt
1/2 cup cornstarch
2-2 1/2 cups finely chopped
   pecans

Prepare plum sauce (recipe below). Set aside.

Cut chicken into finger-size strips. Mix together sherry and mustard; coat chicken with mixture. Sprinkle pieces with salt and pepper, set aside.

Using an electric beater, set at high speed, beat egg whites until foamy. Gradually add cornstarch; continue beating until stiff peaks form. Gently fold in chicken.

Roll each piece of chicken in chopped pecans. Fry in at least 2 inches of hot oil (350°) until golden brown. Remove from heat and drain on paper towels.

Serve chicken pieces with Gingered Plum sauce for dipping. Makes 4 servings.

Gingered Plum Sauce

Heat 1 cup plum jam in a small saucepan over medium heat until melted. Stir in 1 tbs. ketchup, 2 tsp. grated lemon rind, 1 tbs. lemon juice, 2 tsps. vinegar, 1/2 tsp. ground ginger, 1/2 tsp. anise seeds, crushed (may omit), 1/4 tsp. dry mustard, 1/2 tsp. ground cinnamon, 1/8 tsp. ground cloves and 1/8 tsp. hot pepper sauce. Bring to a boil and cook 1 minute, stirring constantly. Remove mixture from heat and let cool.

Makes 1-1/2 cups.

MEXICAN CHICKEN RICE SKILLET

1/2 cup mayonnaise
3/4 cup rice, uncooked
1/2 tsp. cumin
1 cup chicken broth
1 tbs. chili powder
1 medium tomato, chopped
1 4 oz. can chopped green chilies, drained
3 chicken breasts, split, boned, skinned
1/3 cup pitted ripe black olive slices
1/2 cup (2 oz.) Shredded Sharp Cheddar Cheese

In 10 inch skillet, combine mayonnaise, broth, rice, chilies, chill powder and cumin; mix well. Top with chicken. Bring to boil; reduce heat. Cover; simmer 25 minutes. Top with tomatoes and olives. Cover; continue cooking 5 minutes. Remove from heat. Sprinkle with cheese; let stand 5 minutes or until all liquid is absorbed. Serves 3-4.

COUNTRYSIDE CHICKEN BAKE

1 cup uncooked rice
3/4 cup chopped onions
1/2 tsp. salt
1 1/4 cups water
1 cup celery slices
2 tsp. parsley flakes
1/8 tsp. pepper
3/4 cup mayonnaise
1 10-3/4 oz. can condensed cream of mushroom soup
3 chicken breasts, split, skinned

Place rice in greased 12 x 8 inch baking dish. Cover with combined vegetables and seasonings. Combine soup and mayonnaise; mix well. Gradually add water to soup mixture, mixing until well blended. Pour half the soup mixture over vegetables; top with chicken and remaining soup mixture.

Bake at 350° for 1 hour or until chicken is tender and rice is cooked. Sprinkle with paprika, if desired.

SUZY'S OVEN-BAKED CHICKEN

Tastes like fried chicken without the calories.

1 large chicken, cut-up
1 can evaporated milk
2 sups corn flake crumbs
Salt and pepper to taste

Wash and clean chicken. Dip each piece of chicken into the evaporated milk; then thoroughly coat with corn flake crumbs. Put on cookie sheet and bake in a preheated 350 degree oven until done, approximately 1 hour.

BAKED CHICKEN PARMESAN

1 2 1/2-3 lb. broiler-fryer, cut-up, skinned
3/4 cup Light mayonnaise
1 cup cornflake crumbs
1/2 cup (2 oz.) Grated Parmesan Cheese
Dash of salt and pepper

Brush chicken with salad dressing; coat with combined remaining ingredients. Place in 13 x 9 inch baking dish. Bake at 350 1 hour or until tender. Serves 3-4.

Variation: Substitute 1 lb. fish fillets for chicken. Reduce mayonnaise to 1/3 cup, crumbs to 1/2 cup and Parmesan cheese to 1/4 cup. Reduce baking time to 30 minutes, or until fish flakes easily.

CHICKEN FLORENTINE

1 broiler/fryer (2 1/2-3 lbs), cut up
3/4 cup water
1 cube chicken bouillon
1/2 lb mushrooms, sliced
1 bag (10 oz) spinach
4 tsp prepared horseradish
butter
1/4 tsp pepper
2 medium lemons
1/2 tsp salt
1/2 cup milk
1 Tbsp flour

About 1 hour before serving:
In 12" skillet over medium heat, melt 3 Tbsp butter; add chicken and cook until browned on all sides. Add water, pepper and bouillon, heat to boiling. Reduce heat to low, cover; simmer 30 minutes or until fork-tender.

Meanwhile, with sharp knife, cut 1 lemon crosswise into thin slices, cut each slice in half; set aside for garnish later. Squeeze remaining lemon to make 1 Tbsp juice. In 4 quart saucepan over medium heat, melt 2 Tbsp butter; add lemon juice, mushrooms and salt. Cook until mushrooms are tender, - stirring occasionally. With slotted spoon, spoon mushrooms into small bowl. Add spinach to liquid remaining in saucepan and cook over

high heat just until wilted, 2-3 minutes, stirring occasionally. Stir in mushrooms; keep warm.

Skim off fat from liquid in skillet. In cup, mix milk and flour; gradually stir mixture and horseradish into liquid in skillet; cook over medium heat until slightly thickened, stirring constantly.

To serve, arrange spinach mixture on platter; top with chicken pieces. Garnish with reserved lemon slices. Pass gravy in bowl to spoon over chicken and spinach. Serves 4.

CHICKEN/SPINACH QUICHE

piecrust mix for 9" piecrust
1 green onion, minced
1 tsp salt
1 cup Swiss cheese, shredded
1 pkg (10 oz) frozen chopped spinach, thawed and squeezed dry
butter
2 cups half-n-half
1/8 tsp pepper
3 eggs
1 can (5-6 3/4 oz) chunk chicken, drained and flaked

About 1 1/2 hours before serving:
Prepare piecrust mix as label directs; use to line 9" pie plate. Spread crust with 1 Tbsp softened butter
Preheat oven to 425 F. In 1 quart saucepan over medium heat, melt 2 Tbsp butter, add green onion and cook until

tender, stirring occasionally. Remove saucepan from heat; set aside.

In medium bowl with wire whisk or fork, mix half-n-half, salt, pepper and eggs; stir in cheese, spinach, chicken and green onion mixture. Pour into piecrust. Bake 15 minutes; turn oven to 325 F and bake another 30 minutes, or until knife inserted in center comes out clean. Serves 6.

ARTICHOKE CHICKEN

2 to 3 lbs. boned chicken
2 cups creamed chicken soup
1 cup mayonnaise
2 jars (6-1/2 oz.) marinated artichokes
2 Tbs. lemon juice
1 Tbs. curry powder
1 cup shredded sharp Cheddar cheese

Arrange artichokes in greased pan. Cover with chicken (cut in strips).

Combine all other ingredients (except cheese). Pour over chicken and artichoke mixture. Cover with cheese.

Bake at 350 F for 45 minutes to 1 hour.

CHICKEN FLORENTINE

1/3 cup mayonnaise
1/2 tsp. salt
1-1/4 cups milk
1/3 cup (1-1/2 oz.) grated Parmesan cheese

1 10 oz. package frozen chopped spinach, thawed, well-drained
2 chicken breasts, split, boned, skinned
3 Tbs. flour
1/8 tsp. ground nutmeg
1 cup cooked rice

Combine mayonnaise, flour, salt, and nutmeg; gradually add milk. Cook, stirring constantly over low heat until thickened. Stir in cheese. Combine 3/4 cup of the mayonnaise mixture, spinach and rice; spread onto bottom of 10 x 6 inch baking dish. Top with chicken. Spoon remaining mayonnaise mixture over chicken. Sprinkle lightly with additional nutmeg. Bake at 350 for 40 minutes, or until chicken is tender.
Serves 4.

CHICKEN BUNDLES OF LOVE

2 whole chicken breasts (split, skinned and boned)
8 oz. mozzarella cheese, grated
4 Tbs. butter
1/2 cup sherry
Pepper to taste
1/2 cup almond paste
1/2 cup bread crumbs
4 toothpicks
1 garlic clove, halved
2 Tbs. chopped parsley

Pound chicken breasts. Spread almond paste on each breast. Sprinkle evenly with cheese and bread crumbs. Then roll up each breast and secure with toothpick. Melt butter in pan and saute garlic for 1 minute. Add chicken to pan and saute 1 to 2 minutes. Place bundles in oiled pan and bake at 350 F for 20 to 25 minutes. When done, add sherry to pan drippings, mix and pour over chicken. Season with pepper and parsley to taste.

GIL'S CHICKEN CORDON BLEU

8 chicken breasts, boneless and skinless
4 slices Canadian bacon
4 slices Swiss cheese
1/2 cup cornstarch
4 Tbs. butter

Pound and flatten chicken breasts. Place slice of bacon on breast. Place slice of cheese on bacon, another breast on cheese and press breasts together. Coat each side of chicken with cornstarch. Melt butter in frying pan and brown each side for 2 to 3 minutes or until done.

CHICKEN IN WINE SAUCE

1 chicken (5 or 6 lbs.)
12 small white onions, peeled
1/2 clove garlic, minced
1 can (3 oz.) sliced mushrooms
1-1/2 cups California claret or any red table wine
1 tsp. Kitchen Bouquet
1 Tbs. fat
3 Tbs. flour
3 sprigs parsley

Cut chicken into serving pieces. Brush with Kitchen Bouquet. Brown in melted fat over moderate heat, about 10 minutes. Remove chicken to casserole. Add onion and garlic to fat in pan; cook over moderate heat 1 minute. Stir in flour. Add wine, contents of can of mushrooms, parsley and 1/2 tsp. salt. Bring to boil, stirring constantly, until sauce thickens.

Pour sauce over chicken and onions; cover tightly. Bake in 350 F oven until chicken and onions are tender (about 1-1/4 hours). Serve hot with cooked rice.

CHICKEN PICCATA

3 Tbs. flour
1/2 tsp. pepper
1 tsp. salt
1/3 cup dry white wine
1 lb. boneless, skinless chicken (if using breasts, cut in half)
3 Tbs. butter
2 Tbs. vegetable oil
1-1/2 tsp. lemon juice

(To save time, use chicken cutlets.)

On plate or piece of waxed paper, combine flour, salt and pepper. Set aside. Place chicken or cutlets between sheets of wax paper and pound each to 1/4 inch thickness (cutlets may already be 1/4 inch thick). Cut each chicken breast in half. Dip chicken into flour mixture, shaking off excess. In heavy skillet, heat 2 Tbs. butter and vegetable oil until butter is melted. Add chicken and brown slightly on each side. Place chicken on serving plate and keep warm. Add wine and lemon juice to skillet. Cook about 2 minutes, stirring and scraping up any bits, until slightly thickened. Remove from heat and swirl in remaining butter. Pour sauce over chicken and serve immediately.
Serves 4.

PARMESAN CHICKEN

1/4 cup fine dry bread
  crumbs
dash of garlic powder
dash of pepper
1 can cream of chicken soup
paprika
4 Tbs. grated Parmesan
  cheese
1/4 tsp. oregano
2 lbs. chicken parts
1/2 cup milk

Combine crumbs, 2 Tbs. Parmesan cheese, oregano, garlic and pepper; roll chicken in mixture. Arrange in 2 2quart shallow backing dish (12 x 8 x 2). Bake at 400 F for 20 minutes. Turn chicken. Bake 20 minutes more. Meanwhile blend soup and milk; pour over chicken. Sprinkle with paprika and remaining Parmesan cheese. Bake 20 minutes more until done.

BATTER-FRIED CHICKEN

(Excellent with shrimp, too!)

1 cup all purpose flour
1 cup beer
1 broiler-fryer chicken, cut up
  (2 1/2-3 pounds)
Vegetable oil for deep frying
salt
1/4 tsp. pepper

In medium bowl, combine flour, 1 tsp. salt and pepper. Add beer, stirring with wire whisk until smooth. Let stand at room temperature 15 minutes to 1 hour. Meanwhile, lightly sprinkle chicken pieces with salt.

In deep-fat fryer or Dutch oven, heat 2 inches oil to 375 F on deep-fat thermometer. Dip chicken pieces in beer batter, coating on all sides, allowing excess batter to drain back into bowl. Fry chicken legs, thighs, and back 20-25 minutes or until golden brown and cooked through. Drain on paper towels. Keep warm in 200 F oven. Fry breast and wings about 15-20 minutes; drain on paper towels.

Hint: Add some pancake mix to the flour, even when making french-fried onion rings - it gives the chicken, shrimp, etc., crispiness and crunch!

CHICKEN SPARERIBS

2 lbs. chicken thighs, skinned
1 to 2 Tbs. vegetable oil
1 clove garlic, crushed
1/2 tsp. crushed red pepper
1/4 tsp. ginger
1/4 cup apple juice
1/3 cup light brown sugar,
  firmly packed
2 Tbs. ketchup
1 Tbs. cider vinegar
1/2 cup water
1/3 cup soy sauce
1 Tbs. cornstarch
1 Tbs. water

Heat oil in a non-stick skillet over a medium-high heat. Add chicken and lightly brown on all sides, turning frequently for about 6 to 7 minutes. Combine 1/2 cup water, soy sauce, brown sugar, apple juice, ketchup, vinegar, garlic, red pepper and ginger in a bowl and mix. Add to chicken. Bring to a boil, cover and reduce heat and simmer for 20 minutes. In a small bowl, blend cornstarch and water. Add to chicken and cook, stirring, until sauce thickens and glazes chicken pieces. Serve warm as an appetizer or as a main course over hot cooked rice. Garnish with sliced green onions if desired.

May substitute wings for thighs if using as an appetizer.

Yield: 4 main dish servings.

CHICKEN MARENGO

4 choice chicken pieces
1/4 tsp. garlic salt
1-1/2 Tbs. vegetable oil
1/3 cup chicken broth (or use chicken bouillon cube or powder dissolved in 1/3 cup water)
2/3 cup canned tomatoes, chopped
1 cup hot cooked rice
2 Tbs. flour
Dash of pepper
1 Tbs. dry white wine
3 Tbs. sour cream
1/2 small bay leaf

Roll chicken in combined flour, garlic, salt and pepper. Brown in oil. Add wine to skillet. Stir to loosen brown particles. Blend any remaining flour with broth, sour cream and tomatoes. Stir into chicken. Add bay leaf. Cover and simmer about 30 minutes or until chicken is tender.

Remove bay leaf. Serve over beds of fluffy rice.

ORANGE CHICKEN

4 pieces chicken breast, skinned, boned
2 oranges, sectioned and pitted
1/2 cup chopped walnuts
Butter or oil for sauteing
1 tsp. cornstarch
1/2 cup sweet sherry
Salt and pepper

Melt butter and quickly brown chicken pieces on both sides over fairly high heat. Sprinkle with salt and pepper. Add orange slices, cover, reduce heat and cook for about 20 minutes. Blend cornstarch and chopped nuts into sherry; pour mixture over chicken. Serve with rice.

APRICOT CHICKEN

8 pieces chicken
1 pkg. onion soup mix
1 bottle creamy Russian dressing

1 jar (10 oz.) apricot preserves
3/4 cup water

Wash and dry chicken. Bring soup and water to boil. Add preserves and dressing. Mix. Pour over chicken and refrigerate 1 hour. Bake at 350 F for 1 hour and 15 minutes, basting often.

CHERRY CHICKEN

2 chickens, cut into serving pieces
1 jar (12 oz.) cherry preserves
1 can (6 oz.) frozen orange juice
1-1/2 cans of water
1 stick butter
1 can sherry

Preheat oven to 350 F. Heat all ingredients in saucepan until well blended. Put chicken, skin side down in roasting pan, covered for 30 minutes. Uncover pan, pour sauce over chicken and bake for about 1 hour. Baste every 15 minutes.

8 FISH & SEAFOOD

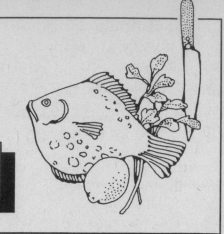

HINTS

Frozen fish need not be thawed before cooking.

If barbecuing fish steaks, first grease the grill. Cooking time is 7 to minutes for the first side, and 5 minutes for the second side. Baste with a sauce while cooking.

To avoid a fishy smell on your hands, when preparing fish, chill it thoroughly in cold water before handling it.

To avoid unpleasant cooking odors while making fish, cover with browned butter or lemon juice.

Do not overcook fish or seafood. Fish is done when it flakes easily.

Serve fish immediately after it is cooked.

RED SNAPPER WITH SPICED CINNAMON CACAO BUTTER SAUCE

Fish:
1 4-5 lb. whole red snapper, scaled and cleaned
1/4 tsp. salt
3 Tbs. dry white wine
1/4 tsp. fresh black pepper
2 Tbs. unsalted butter, soft

Cacao Butter Sauce:
1/3 cup dry white wine
1 sm. shallot, finely chopped
1/2 tsp. ground cinnamon
1/4 cup whipping cream
2 sticks unsalted butter, cut into tablespoons
Lemon wedges, if desired
1/3 cup white wine vinegar
1 tsp. unsweetened cocoa
1/4 tsp. ground red pepper
parsley, for garnish

Prepare the Fish:
Preheat oven to 400. Rub the entire fish with the butter. Place the fish in a shallow oblong baking dish. Sprinkle the fish both on the inside and the outside with salt, pepper, and wine. Cover

with foil, pressing down around the edges.

Bake the fish for 20 minutes. Uncover and bake for 15 minutes longer. Place the fish on a warm serving platter and keep it in a warm place. Strain and reserve the juices from the pan.

Make the Sauce:

In a medium saucepan, combine the reserved juices, wine, vinegar, shallot, cocoa powder, cinnamon, salt and red pepper. Heat over medium high heat until the mixture is reduced to 1-1/2 tablespoons .

Stir in cream and continue cooking until the mixture is reduced by half. One tablespoon at a time, whisk in the butter until it is well incorporated and emulsified. Remove the pan from the heat if the sauce gets too hot. The end result should be a light emulsified sauce, not a pool of liquid butter.

Spoon the sauce over the fish. Garnish with parsley and serve with lemon wedges, if desired.

BAKED SHRIMP WITH SEASONED BREAD CRUMBS

2 lb. large shrimp-shelled, with the last section of the tail shell left intact, and deveined
3/4 cup fresh bread crumbs

5 1/2 tablespoons Red pepper and Herb butter (recipe below) or Tarragon-Pernod Butter (recipe below).
Garlic (optional)

Preheat oven to 500 F. In a large buttered ovenproof serving dish, arrange the shrimp with their tails in the air. Top the flat surface of each shrimp with about 1 tsp. of the bread crumbs and 1/2 tsp. of a flavored butter. Bake for about 5 minutes, or until the shrimp are just opaque throughout.

Red Pepper and Herb Butter
Makes about 10 tablespoons

1/2 red bell pepper, cut into small pieces
2 scallions, chopped
1 tbs. chopped garlic
1/2 tsp. thyme
1 tbs. chopped parsley
Pinch of cayenne pepper
1 stick (1/4 lb.) unsalted butter, cut into pieces

Combine the bell pepper, scallions, garlic, thyme, parsley and cayenne in a food processor. Turn the machine on and off until the ingredients are minced but not pureed. Add the butter pieces and process until blended. Transfer the butter to a sheet of plastic wrap and roll into a log shape about 1 1/2 inches in diameter. Roll up in plastic and twist the ends securely. Freeze the butter until firm, about 1 1/2 hours.

Tarragon-Pernod Butter
This butter can be kept on hand in the freezer for several months. To turn this or the Red Pepper and Herb Butter into a delicious emulsified sauce for roasted shellfish, cut it into pieces and melt slowly over low heat, whisking constantly. When the butter is completely melted and emulsified, transfer to a bowl and serve.

1-1/2 tbs. chopped shallot
1-1/2 tsp. tarragon vinegar
1/2 tsp. coarsely cracked pepper
1-1/2 tsp. tarragon
1 tsp. Pernod
1 stick unsalted butter, cut

Combine the shallot, tarragon, vinegar, Pernod and pepper in a food processor, until minced. Add butter until blended. Roll in a log about 1 1/2 inches in plastic wrap. Roll up in plastic and twist ends securely. Freeze until firm, about 1 1/2 hours.

SAUCY SHRIMP STIR-FRY

2 tbs. oil
1 tsp. finely chopped ginger
1 cup broccoli flowerets
1/2 cup red pepper chunks
3/4 lb. cleaned shrimp
1 tbs. soy sauce
1 cup pea pods
1/2 cup carrots, julienne
1/4 cup green onion slices
1/2 cup light mayonnaise

In wok or large skillet, heat 1 tbs. oil over medium-high heat. Add vegetables. Stir-fry 3-4 minutes or until crisp-tender; remove from pan. Add remaining oil to pan. Add shrimp; stir-fry 3-4 minutes or until pink. Return vegetables to pan. Remove from heat. Add combined mayonnaise, soy sauce and ginger; mix well. Serve hot over cooked rice.

Variation: May substitute chicken, cubed instead of shrimp.

CAJUN BAKED FISH

1/3 cup mayonnaise
1/2 tsp. onion powder
1/4 tsp. garlic powder
1/2 cup crushed sesame
  crackers
1/2 tsp. cumin
1/4 tsp. ground red pepper
1 lb. fish fillets

Combine mayonnaise and seasonings. Brush fish with this mixture; coat with crumbs. Place in greased 13 x 9 inch baking dish. Bake at 350 for 30 minutes or until fish flakes easily. Serves 3 or 4.

BAKED FISH WITH HERB SAUCE

1/4 cup mayonnaise
1/4 tsp. salt
1/2 cup milk
1/2 tsp. lemon juice
1 lb. fish fillets
1 tbs. flour
Dash of pepper
2 tbs. chopped parsley
1/4 tsp. basil
Salt and Pepper

Combine mayonnaise, flour, salt and pepper. Gradually add milk; cook, stirring constantly, over medium-low heat until thickened. Stir in parsley, lemon juice and basil.

Place fish in greased shallow baking dish; season with salt and pepper. Bake at 350 for 10 min. Serve with mayonnaise mixture.

CAPTAIN'S CHOICE

2 lbs Spanish mackerel fillets
1 tsp salt
1/4 tsp pepper
1 Tbsp melted butter
1/2 cup mayonnaise
2 Tbsp catsup
2 tsp prepared mustard

Sprinkle fish with salt and pepper. Place fish, skin side down on a well-greased broiler pan. Baste with butter. Broil approximately 4" from source of heat for 8-10 minutes. Combine mayonnaise, catsup and mustard. Spread mixture evenly over fish. Broil 4-5 minutes longer or until sauce bubbles and is lightly browned.

BAKED SNAPPER FILLETS

2 lbs snapper fillets
2 Tbsp finely chopped onion
1 can (10 3/4 oz) condensed
  cream of tomato soup
1 tsp salt
1/4 tsp pepper
1 cup grated Swiss cheese

Sprinkle fish with salt and pepper. Place fillets in a well-greased baking pan (approximately 12" x 8" x 2"). Combine soup and onion. Spread over fish. Sprinkle with cheese. Bake in 350 F oven for 25-30 minutes or until fish flakes easily when tested with fork.

GROUPER PARMESAN

2 lbs grouper fillets
1/4 cup grated Parmesan
  cheese
1 Tbsp grated onion
1/8 tsp liquid hot sauce
chopped parsley
1 cup sour cream
1 Tbsp lemon juice
1/2 tsp salt paprika

Skin fillets and cut into serving size portions. Place in a well-greased baking dish 12" x 8" x 2". Combine sour cream, Parmesan cheese, lemon juice, onion, salt and liquid hot sauce. Spread sour cream mixture over fish. Sprinkle with paprika. Bake in 350 F oven for 25-30 minutes or until fish flakes easily. Garnish with parsley.

TROTELLE ALLA SAVOIA (BAKED TROUT WITH MUSHROOMS)

1/2 large trout per person, filleted
Salt
Freshly ground black pepper
Flour
9 Tbs. butter, divided
7 scallions, thinly sliced (white part & 2-3 inches of green)
1/2 cup fresh white bread crumbs (whirl slices in blender)
3 Tbs. olive oil
1-1/4 pounds fresh mushrooms, thinly sliced
2 Tbs. lemon juice

Preheat oven to 425 degrees. Wash the trout fillets under cold water and pat them dry with paper towels. Season the fillets lightly with salt and pepper, then roll them in flour and brush or shake off the excess.

In a heavy skillet, melt 3 Tbs. of butter with the olive oil over high heat. When the foam subsides, add the trout, skin side up and cook for 2 minutes on each side or until they are golden brown. Carefully transfer the trout to a platter.

In a stainless steel or enameled skillet, melt another 3 Tbs. of butter over high heat. Add the sliced mushrooms, sprinkle them with lemon juice, and while shaking the skillet almost constantly, cook for about 3 minutes, or until they glisten with butter and are slightly softened, but not sauteed. With a slotted spoon, remove the mushrooms from the skillet and spread them over the bottom of a buttered oven-proof baking dish just large enough to hold the trout in one layer.

Melt 1 Tbs. of butter in the skillet, add the scallions and cook them for 1 minute. Then with a slotted spoon transfer them to a bowl. In the remaining 2 Tbs. of butter, and the same skillet, lightly brown the bread crumbs.

Arrange the browned trout, adding any juices that have accumulated on the platter, on top of the mushrooms in the baking dish. Sprinkle them with the crisp bread crumbs and spread the scallions on top.

These may be made ahead. When ready to serve, bake on the middle rack of the oven for 10 minutes, or until the crumbs and scallions are brown. Serve directly from the baking dish.
Serves 10-12.

BROILED HALIBUT WITH ALMOND BUTTER

1 Tbs. chopped shallots
1/3 cup sliced almonds
1/2 tsp. crushed basil
20 medium fresh asparagus stalks, trimmed and blanched
2 Tbs. butter
1 Tbs. lemon juice
4 halibut steaks (4-6 oz.)

Saute shallots in butter until tender; stir in almonds, lemon juice and basil. Place halibut on well greased broiler pan. Brush fish with butter mixture. Place in oven 4 inches below broiler.

Broil, allowing 10 minutes per inch of thickness measured at its thickest part turn steaks halfway through cooking and brush again with butter mixture.

Spoon nuts from remaining butter mixture onto steaks during the last 2 minutes of cooking. Cook until halibut flakes with a fork. Serve over bed of asparagus. Makes 4 servings.

POACHED SALMON STEAKS WITH SALSA

These delicious salmon steaks are great as either a hot or cold entree.

1 cup salsa (recipe follows)
2-1/2 cups water
1/2 cup dry vermouth or white wine
1/4 cup lemon juice
2 tsp. salt
4 1/2-inch-thick salmon steaks (about 1 1/2 lbs. total)

In a large skillet over high heat, bring water, vermouth, lemon juice and salt to a brisk simmer. Add salmon steaks. Cover. Simmer 6-8 minutes or until salmon turns from translucent to opaque .

With a slotted spatula, transfer each steak to a serving plate. Serve with salsa.

Salsa
3/4 cup mild or hot salsa
2 Tbs. lemon juice

To prepare salsa, pour it into a small bowl and stir in lemon juice. Set aside.

WONDERFUL SEAFOOD PIE

1 pkg. (6 oz.) frozen crabmeat or shrimp*, thawed and drained, or 1 can (6-1/2 oz.) tuna, drained
1 cup shredded American cheese
1 pkg. (3 oz.) cream cheese, cut into 1/4 inch cubes
1 jar (2 oz.) chopped pimento, drained - optional
1/4 cup sliced green onions
2 cups milk
1 cup Bisquick baking mix
4 eggs
1/4 tsp. salt
Dash of nutmeg

Heat oven to 400 F. Grease 10" pie plate. Mix crabmeat, cheese, onions and pimento in plate. Beat remaining ingredients until smooth - 15 seconds in blender on high, or 1 minute with hand beater. Pour into plate. Bake until knife inserted between center and edge comes out clean, 35 to 40 minutes. Cool 5 minutes.

*1 can (6 oz.) crabmeat, drained and cartilage removed, or 1 can (4-1/2 oz.) shrimp, well-drained and rinsed can be substituted for the frozen crabmeat or shrimp.

Serves 6 to 8.

TRISH'S TUNA CASSEROLE

2 cans cream of mushroom soup
1 can cream of celery soup
1 can corn, drained
1 can peas, drained
1 large can mushrooms
garlic powder
cooking sherry
1 lb. Velveeta cheese
egg noodles
2 large cans tuna

Cook noodles. Mix soups with tuna; mix in mushrooms, peas and corn. Add 1/4 to 1/2 cup cooking sherry. Add noodles. Put mixture into casserole. Cut Velveeta cheese into strips 1/4 inch thick; push strips into mixture approximately 1 inch apart. Cover with Carnation Evaporated Milk, barely enough to cover top. Bake at 325 F for 1 hour. Before coming out, crumble potato chips over top.

MONTY'S CRAB CAKES

1 lb. back fin crab meat
1 whole egg, beaten
1 Tbs. chopped parsley
1-1/2 tsp. Dijon mustard
1/4 tsp. ground white pepper
1/2 cup bread crumbs
1/2 cup mayonnaise
2 tsp. Worcestershire sauce
1 tsp. salt

Mix all ingredients except crab meat. Add crab and toss lightly. Chill for at least 1 hour. pat into 6 (4 oz.) cakes and dust with flour. Saute in clarified butter over medium heat until golden brown on each side. Serve hot.

CATCH OF THE DAY

9 VEGETABLES
& HINTS

HINTS

Fresh mushrooms should be cooked immediately after washing. They should also be used as soon as possible after buying. One pound of fresh mushrooms equals six ounces of canned mushrooms.

For crisp carrots: add a little sugar to cold water.

Peel carrots under water, and they will not stain your fingers.

Onions won't cause tears if they are well chilled. Store in covered containers in the refrigerator.

To keep dill fresh: store in a tightly closed jar in the refrigerator. It will keep about a month.

To eliminate odor when cooking cabbage: drop a whole walnut into the boiling water.

Leave a one inch stem on beets when cooking to minimize bleeding.

For crisp celery: let stand in ice water for a few minutes before serving.

To reheat cooked rice: fill pan with just enough water to cover bottom. Spoon in rice and steam about 5 minutes, until water is absorbed and rice is fluffy again.

Rice will be extra white by adding 2 teaspoons of lemon juice before cooking.

To prevent grease-soaked potatoes, boil until nearly tender, then add to roast for 30 minutes until brown.

Grate potatoes directly into a bowl of cold water to prevent them from turning dark. Drain off water before potatoes are used.

Leftover boiled potatoes may be sliced and browned in hot oil.

When baking potatoes: always prick skin with a fork to let steam escape. Greasing them before baking will keep the skins soft.

Add a teaspoon of baking powder to potatoes before mashing and beat vigorously. They will be light and fluffy.

Cut baking time in half for potatoes by boiling them first for 15 minutes.

Add 1 tablespoon oil to water when boiling pasta to prevent it from sticking together and to prevent the water from boiling over.

COOKING TIME FOR VEGETABLES

Asparagus:
(whole)	1 inch boiling salted water, covered	15-20 min.
(pieces)	1 inch boiling salted water, covered	10-15 min.
(tips)	1 inch boiling salted water, covered	5-10 min.

Green or Wax Beans:
(whole)	1 inch boiling salted water, covered	15-20 min.
(pieces)	1 inch boiling salted water, covered	15-20 min.
(strips	1 inch boiling salted water, covered	10 min.

Lima Beans:
(whole)	1 inch boiling salted water, covered	20-25 min.

Beets:
(whole)	1 inch boiling salted water, covered	30-40 min.
(sliced)	1 inch boiling salted water, covered	15-20 min.
(shredded)	1 inch boiling salted water, covered	8 min.
OR	bake covered at 350° in 1/4 inch water	45-60 min.

Broccoli: 1 inch boiling salted water, covered,
ends down, and heads out of water — 10-15 min.

Brussel Sprouts:
(whole)	1 inch boiling salted water, covered	8-10 min.

Cabbage:
(wedges)	1 inch boiling salted water, covered	20-30 min.
(shredded)	1/4 inch boiling salted water, covered	5-8 min.

Carrots:
(whole)	1 inch boiling salted water, covered	20-30 min.
(sliced)	1 inch boiling salted water, covered	15-25 min.
(shredded)	1/4 inch boiling salted water, covered	5-7 min.
OR	bake covered at 350° in 1/4 inch water	50-60 min.

Cauliflower:
(whole)	1 inch boiling salted water, covered	20-30 min.
(flowerets)	1 inch boiling salted water, covered	10-15 min.
	(add salt later, for white color)	

Corn: unsalted water to cover, plus 1 tsp. — 5-8 min.
sugar (add salt later for tender corn)

Eggplant: bake at 350°, uncovered, until tender — 45-60 min.
OR broil 8-10 min. per side, until tender

Mushrooms: Sauté in butter — 8-10 min.
OR broil — 5-8 min.

Onions:
(whole)	1 inch boiling salted water, covered	30-35 min.
(sliced)	1 inch boiling salted water, covered	15-20 min.
OR	sauté in butter or oil	8-10 min.

Peas: 1 inch boiling salted water, covered — 10-12 min.
(add pods and a little sugar for flavor)

Potatoes:
(whole)	1 inch boiling water, covered	30-35 min.
(sliced)	1 inch boiling water, covered	15-20 min.
OR	bake at 425 degrees	45-60 min.
OR	fry in deep fat at 375°	5-7 min.

Tomatoes: bake at 375° — 25 min.
OR broil — 5 min.

HERBED BAKED TOMATOES

3 Tbs. seasoned dry bread crumbs
2 Tbs. butter or margarine, melted
2 Tbs. grated Parmesan cheese
1/2 tsp. oregano or basil
2 medium tomatoes, cut in half

Combine bread crumbs, butter, cheese and oregano. Set oven broiling rack in upper rack guides. Place tomato halves on spatter shield; top with bread crumb mixture. Place broiler pan on oven broiling rack. Cook on Broil, 14-15 minutes, or until tomatoes are tender.

Microwave method:

Arrange tomato halves in 8 inch square dish; top with bread crumb mixture. Cover with plastic wrap. Cook on High, 1-1/2 to 2 minutes, or until tomatoes are tender. Let stand, covered, 2 minutes.
Yield: 4 servings

GREEN PEAS WITH MUSHROOMS

3 Tbs. butter or margarine
2 Tbs. finely grated yellow onion
1/2 lb. button mushrooms, stems trimmed, wiped clean and thinly sliced
2 bags (20 oz. each) frozen green peas (do not thaw)
1/2 tsp. leaf rosemary, crumbled
1/4 tsp. ground nutmeg
1/2 tsp. salt
1/4 tsp. pepper

Melt butter in very large, heavy skillet over medium-high heat. Add onion and mushrooms; sauté 3 to 4 minutes until mushroom juices have evaporated.
Rap bags of peas against counter to break up frozen clumps. Add peas to skillet along with rosemary and nutmeg. Lower heat to medium. Cover skillet and cook 4 minutes.
Stir well. Cook, uncovered, 4 to 6 minutes longer until peas are heated through. Season with salt and pepper.

SQUASH SOUFFLE

2 lbs. fresh yellow squash, chopped
2 eggs, beaten
2 Tbs. sugar
1 small onion, chopped
Pepper to taste
1 (15-1/3 oz.) can evaporated milk
1/4 lb. Cheddar cheese, grated
1 tsp. salt
3/4 cup ground potato chips or crackers
2 Tbs. melted butter
(no substitutes)

Steam squash and onions together until tender. Place in a bowl and add milk, salt, butter, eggs, sugar, pepper and cheese. Mix until well blended and place in a greased 8x10 inch pan. Top with potato chips or crackers. Bake in a preheated, 325° oven for 45 minutes.
Yield: 12 servings

STONE CRAB'S GRILLED TOMATOES

4 beefsteak tomatoes
3/4 cup melted butter
2 cups creamed spinach (your favorite recipe)
Salt and pepper to taste
1-1/2 cups grated mild Cheddar cheese
3 cups seasoned bread crumbs

Cut each tomato into 3 thick slices and arrange on an oiled baking sheet. Combine creamed spinach with bread crumbs, butter, salt and pepper. (The mixture should be thick.) Spread each tomato slice with the spinach mixture and sprinkle with grated cheese. Place the tomatoes under a broiler and cook until the cheese is melted and golden brown.
Yield: 4 to 6 servings

BEER BATTER FRIED ZUCCHINI

2 large zucchini
Pinch of salt
2 cups self-rising flour
Pinch of white pepper
5 Tbs. butter, melted
Pinch of garlic salt
2 eggs

4 drops lemon juice
8 oz. regular domestic beer
Oil for deep-frying

Wash zucchini and slice 1/4 inch thick on the diagonal; cover and set aside. In an electric mixer, mix flour with butter and eggs. Add beer, mixing until combined. Add spices and lemon juice and mix for about 10 minutes. Heat oil in a deep-fryer until hot. Hand-dip zucchini in batter and deep-fry in oil for about 3 to 5 minutes until it turns golden brown.
Yield: 4 servings

BAKED CAULIFLOWER

1 whole cauliflower
Margarine
Ritz cracker crumbs

Wash and trim cauliflower. Smear margarine all over cauliflower and dip vegetable in cracker crumbs. Bake whole at 350° for 10 to 15 minutes.

SCRUMPTIOUS BAKED CARROTS

1/4 to 1/2 cup oil
3 garlic cloves, chopped
1 onion, chopped
1/2 tsp. oregano
2 tsp. Mrs. Dash
2 tsp. Salad Supreme

Cut carrots into 1 inch slices. Mix all ingredients together. Marinate carrots overnight. Drain oil, retaining the spices. Bake at 375° for 1 hour, or until carrots are brown and crispy.

CORN SOUFFLE

2 cans cream style corn
3 eggs
1-1/2 bags low-salt saltines, crumbled
1/2 cup milk, whole or skim
1 to 1-1/2 cups sugar, white or brown

Mix all ingredients together and put in casserole dish. Put thin pats of butter on top of mixture. Bake at 350° for 50 to 60 minutes.

PICKLED OKRA

8 lbs. okra
1/2 clove garlic
1/2 tsp. ground pepper or 4 or 5 whole peppers (hot)
1 Tbs. dill seed or fresh dill
1 qt. white vinegar
1 cup water
1/2 cup salt (or less)
2 Tbs. alum

Cover okra with cold water and let stand about 3 hours. Drain and pack in pint jars.
Heat remaining ingredients together. Bring to a boil and pour over packed okra, seal and set stand for two weeks.

LENTIL ROAST

1-1/2 cups red lentils
2 cups water
1 cup chopped onion
1 clove garlic, chopped
1/4 cup vegetable oil
1-1/2 cups grated cheese
1 egg, beaten
1 tsp. parsley flakes
1/4 tsp. thyme
1 tsp. salt
Dash nutmeg

Simmer lentils until soft (about 25 minutes). Do not drain the beans. Sauté onions and garlic in oil until lightly browned. Mix together all ingredients and put in an oiled dish.
Bake at 375° for 35 to 40 minutes. Serve with gravy.

HUMMUS-SESAME SPREAD

1 can (l lb.) garbanzo beans, drained
1/2 cup lemon juice
1/2 cup tahini paste
3 Tbs. finely chopped onion
2 cloves garlic, peeled and minced
Salt and pepper

Place beans, lemon juice, tahini, onions and garlic in a food processor or blender. Blend until smooth. Add salt and pepper to taste, blend again. Chill. Great as a dip or sandwich spread for pita bread.
Yield: 2 cups

CORN PUDDING I

2 cans (17 oz. each) whole
    kernel corn
1 can (17 oz.) cream-style
    corn
1 sleeve saltine crackers,
    crushed
2 drops vanilla extract
1/4 cup brown sugar
6 eggs, well beaten
Dash pepper
Dash ground cinnamon or
nutmeg, optional

Preheat oven to 350°. In a
large bowl combine all the
ingredients. Mix well. Place
in 2-1/2 quart soufflé or
casserole dish that has been
coated with nonstick veg-
etable spray. Bake 1 hour or
until golden brown and set.

CORN PUDDING II

1 can (17 oz.) whole kernel
    corn
1 can (17 oz.) cream-style corn
2 eggs, beaten
1/4 cup milk
1/4 cup sugar
2 Tbs. cornstarch

Preheat oven to 350°. Coat
1-1/2 or 2 quart casserole
with nonstick vegetable
spray.
In a large bowl, combine all
the ingredients. Mix well.
Place in casserole and bake
for 70 minutes or until gold-
en brown and set.

BOURBON CARROTS

1-1/2 lbs. carrots, peeled
1 Tbs. granulated sugar
3-1/2 Tbs. sweet butter
    (divided use)
1/2 tsp. salt, plus more if
needed
1-1/2 cuts water
Freshly ground pepper to
taste
2 Tbs. dark brown sugar
2 Tbs. bourbon
1-1/2 Tbs. chopped fresh
parsley, for garnish

Cut the carrots on the diagonal into 1/4 inch slices. In a
heavy saucepan, combine the
carrots, granulated sugar, 1-
1/2 Tbs. of the butter and 1/2
tsp. salt. Add the water and
bring to a boil. Reduce the
heat to a simmer and cover.
Cook until the carrots are tender when pierced with a
knife, 10-15 minutes. Drain
the carrots, taste and add
more salt if needed. Add the
pepper.
Melt the remaining 2 Tbs.
butter with the brown sugar
in a heavy skillet over medium-high heat. When the
sugar has dissolved, add the
carrots, and sauté until they
are well coated and heated
through. Add the bourbon
and cook 2-3 minutes.
Garnish with parsley.
Yield: 6 servings

Note:
Carrots may be cooked several hours before serving
time and kept covered at
room temperature. Carefully
reheat over medium heat
before serving.

SPINACH-ARTICHOKE CASSEROLE

3 pkgs. frozen chopped
spinach, cooked and drained
1 can artichoke hearts, cut
and drained
1 can Cream of Mushroom
soup
1 cup shredded Mozzarella
cheese
Parmesan cheese
1 garlic clove to taste

Mix all ingredients. Put in
casserole and bake at 350°
until the cheese is melted and
it is hot.
May be prepared and
frozen in advance. If freezing, do not bake until
defrosted and ready to serve.

BLACK BEANS A LA VALDES-FAULI

2 lbs. dried black beans
4 to 5 medium onions, peeled
    and chopped
1 medium-sized green pep-
    per, seeded and chopped
4 or 5 garlic cloves, peeled
    and minced
1 (4-1/2 oz.) can sweet red
    peppers, minced (save
    juice)
1 to 1-1/2 cups olive oil
1 (8 oz.) can tomato sauce
Salt and pepper to taste
2 tsp. white vinegar

1 tsp. sugar
Sweet red pepper strips for
   garnish

The night before you plan to make the dish, wash the beans in one or two changes of water, picking out the broken beans. Put them in a large, heavy pot and cover them with cold water. Let them soak overnight. Using the same water, start cooking them over low heat for two or three hours, until they soften. Skim the foam that rises to the top. You may need to add hot water during the cooking to prevent sticking and burning.

Chop the onions and green pepper; peel and mince the garlic cloves; mince the red peppers. In a large skillet, cook the garlic, onions and green pepper in their own juices and about 1 cup of olive oil (almost enough to cover them), over low heat, for about 15 minutes.

Add the red peppers and cook about 5 minutes over low heat. Add half the can of tomato sauce. Cook 10 more minutes.

When beans are soft, stir in the pepper-tomato mixture and let everything cook over a low heat about 10 or 15 minutes, until the mixture thickens, stirring occasionally.

Then add salt and pepper to taste. Continue cooking about 30 minutes. Add white vinegar and sugar. Add olive oil to taste. Stir frequently, so the beans won't stick to the bottom of the pot.

Garnish with strips of sweet red peppers.

Yield: 12 servings

VEGETABLE BRUNCH PIE

1 pkg. (10 oz.) frozen chopped broccoli or chopped spinach, or 1 pkg. (8 oz.) frozen asparagus spears, cooked and drained
1 cup sour cream
1/4 cup Parmesan cheese
1/2 cup Bisquick baking mix
1/4 cup melted butter
2 eggs
1 tomato, peeled and thinly sliced
1 cup creamed cottage cheese

Heat oven to 350°. Grease 9 inch pie plate. Spread broccoli in plate. Beat sour cream, cottage cheese, baking mix, butter and eggs until smooth, 15 seconds in blender on high or 1 minute with hand beater. Pour into pie plate. Top with tomatoes; sprinkle with parmesan cheese. Bake until knife inserted between center and edge comes out clean, about 30 minutes. Cool 5 minutes.

Yield: 6 to 8 servings

BROCCOLI ALLA ROMANA

1/2 cup olive oil
3 cups dry white wine
2 tsp. garlic, finely chopped

Salt and freshly ground pepper
10 to 12 cups fresh broccoli flowerets (about 4 lbs. fresh)

In a heavy 10 to 12 inch skillet, heat olive oil until a light haze forms over it. Remove pan from heat and stir in garlic. Stir for 30 seconds. Return to medium heat and toss broccoli flowerets in oil until they glisten. Add wine, salt and a few grindings of pepper. Continuing to simmer, uncovered, stirring occasionally, for 5 minutes. Next, cover skillet and simmer for another 15 minutes or until broccoli is tender.

To serve, quickly transfer flowerets with slotted spoon to heated bowl or deep platter. Briskly boil liquid left in skillet over high heat until it has reduced to about 1 cup and pour over broccoli.

Yield: 10 to 12 servings

BROCCOLI BENEDICT

Prepare a 10 oz. pkg. of frozen Welsh rarebit according to package directions.

Split, toast and butter two English muffins. Cook a 10 oz. pkg. frozen broccoli spears according to directions. Drain.

Heat 4 slices Canadian bacon. Top each muffin half with one slice bacon, broccoli spears and 4 to 5 Tbs. rarebit.

SAUTEED BROCCOLI WITH GARLIC

2 Tbs. vegetable oil
1 garlic clove, chopped
2 Tbs. olive oil
1/4 tsp. crushed red pepper
1 bunch broccoli, trimmed
   and cut into small flowerets

In heavy skillet heat oils, add garlic and crushed red pepper. Add broccoli and turn to coat by shaking pan or tossing broccoli with spoon. Sauté over medium heat for 7 to 9 minutes or until broccoli is tender but still crisp. Sprinkle with salt to taste.
   Yield: 4 servings

ORIENTAL BROCCOLI

1 medium onion
1 Tbs. soy sauce
1 Tbs. oil
1 cup bean sprouts
1 pkg. (10 oz.) frozen broccoli
   spears, halved crosswise

In medium saucepan, sauté onion in oil until translucent. Add broccoli spears and soy sauce; cover and cook 5 minutes. Stir in bean sprouts; heat through.

BROCCOLI 'N' MUSHROOM BAKE

1/2 cup mayonnaise
3 Tbs. flour
1/4 tsp. salt
1 Tbs. butter
1 can mushrooms, drained
2 Tbs. sliced pimento,
   drained
1/4 cup crushed wheat crackers
1/8 tsp. pepper
1 cup milk
2 pkgs. (10 oz.) frozen broccoli spears, cooked, and drained

Combine mayonnaise, flour and seasonings. Gradually add milk; cook, stirring constantly, over low heat until thickened. Remove from heat; stir in mushrooms and pimento. Arrange broccoli in a 12x8 inch baking dish; top with mayonnaise mixture. Toss crumbs with butter; sprinkle over casserole. Bake at 350° for 25 to 30 minutes or until thoroughly heated.
   Yield: 6 to 8 servings

Make ahead:
   Prepare as directed except for baking. Cover; refrigerate several hours or overnight. When ready to serve, bake uncovered at 350° for 30 minutes or until thoroughly heated.

BROCCOLI SUPREME

2 pkgs. frozen broccoli spears
1 can Cream of Mushroom
   soup
1 can french fried onion rings
2/3 cup evaporated milk
1 cup grated American
   cheese

Prepare broccoli according to package, cooking only for 5 minutes. Drain; put into greased 2 quart baking dish. Sprinkle with cheese. Bake at 350° for 25 minutes. Remove from oven. Top with onion rings. Bake for 8 to 10 minutes longer, or until onions are crisp and golden brown.
   Yield: 6 to 8 servings

RICE AND BROCCOLI CASSEROLE

1 chopped onion
1 cup Cream of Mushroom
   soup
1 pkg. frozen broccoli
1 cup Minute Rice, uncooked
1/2 stick butter
1/4 cup water
1/2 cup Cheez Whiz
1/2 cup milk

Cook and drain broccoli; set aside. Meanwhile, sauté onion in butter. Add rest of ingredients. Bake in ungreased casserole uncovered for 30 to 40 minutes at 350°.

10 EGGS
& CHEESES

HINTS

To boil a cracked egg: wrap it in aluminum foil and boil.

For greatest volume when beating egg whites: let them stand at room temperature before beating.

To separate the white from the yolk: it is much easier when the egg is cold.

To prevent eggs from cracking when cooking: let them stand at room temperature first.

To stop cooking process: cool boiled eggs immediately under cold running water. Remove shell.

Store eggs large end up. Use in 2 weeks. Hard boiled eggs will keep 1 week.

Grate dry cheese and keep in a covered container. Excellent for cooking.

Grate cheese immediately upon removal from refrigerator. It is much easier.

Soft cheese such as Camembert or Brie should not be kept long, and should be taken out of the refrigerator an hour before serving.

Cutting cheese from center and pushing edges together prevents cheese from drying.

Wrap cheese in a cloth sprinkled with vinegar. It won't pickle it, but it will keep it from hardening.

Sour cream will keep up to 2 weeks. Store it upside down.

Soak pans in hot water after use, but for eggs, milk or cooked cereal that sticks, soak in cold water.

Pasteurized and homogenized milk can be frozen up to 2 weeks in original container. Allow 2 inch air space for expansion.

To keep pancakes hot, cover with a colander. Holes let steam out, so pancakes stay

warm but not limp.

When making a big batch of French Toast, bake at 500 ° for 10 to 12 minutes, until browned, on a well-greased cookie sheet.

Egg whites may be frozen for several months. Place egg whites in a plastic container or an ice cube tray for easy storing.

To keep egg whites from disintegrating while poaching, add one teaspoon vinegar to the water.

Raw egg yolks keep up to 3 days if covered with cold water before storing in refrigerator.

Egg whites should be room temperature before beating stiff.

To hard cook eggs, place them in cold water, bring to a boil, then turn off heat and leave eggs in covered saucepan on stove burner for

15 minutes. Immediately plunge eggs into ice water for easy peeling.

Before grating cheese, rub small amount of salad oil on the grater or processor blade. The cheese won't stick.

To keep mold off cheese, wipe cheese with vinegar and put 2 sugar cubes in with cheese in airtight container.

Cottage cheese will keep longer if the container is inverted when storing in the refrigerator.

EASTER EGG HINTS

The fresher the egg, the harder it is to peel. For best results, buy eggs a week or so ahead of the time you plan to cook them.

The gray-green ring around the yolk comes from a reaction between the iron and the sulfur in the egg. It doesn't affect the taste, but if you'd rather avoid it, don't boil eggs and do cool them quickly.

If neatness counts in your house, invest a few dollars in an egg slicer. To use it to chop eggs, just reverse the sliced egg in the tray and slice again.

If you are concerned about reports of salmonella bacteria in eggs, remember that it is killed by thorough cooking.

Though salmonella outbreaks have largely been limited to New England and the Mid-Atlantic states, wary eaters should avoid dishes that use uncooked or lightly cooked eggs - homemade mayonnaise, Caesar salad dressing and the like. The risk is greater for the elderly, pregnant women, the very young and those whose immune systems are impaired.

HOW TO HARD-COOK EGGS

Notice that "hard-boil" has given way to "hard-cook." Boiling is what makes eggs tough and rubbery. These directions are from the American Egg Board:

Place eggs in a single layer in saucepan.

Add enough water to come at least 1 inch above eggs.

Cover pan and quickly bring to a boil.

Turn off heat. If necessary, remove pan from heat to prevent further boiling.

Let eggs stand covered, in hot water 15 to 17 minutes for large eggs.

Immediately run cold water over eggs or place them in ice water until completely cooled.

To remove shells, tap it gently all over to crack. Roll egg between hands to loosen shell, then peel, starting at large end. Hold under cold running water or dip in bowl of water to ease off shell.

EGG-DYEING TIPS

If you're not going to color the eggs right after cooking them, store them in their cartons in the refrigerator.

Don't color or hide cracked eggs.

To color eggs, use water warmer than the eggs and refrigerate in their cartons right after coloring.

In South Florida, it's safer not to eat the same eggs you've colored and hidden. For the rest of the country, do not eat eggs that have been out of the refrigerator for more than 2 hours. It is best to make separate batches for hiding and eating. Or hide the plastic kind of egg, especially if you hide them in the shrubbery while the children are sleeping.

ONION CHEESE PIE

1 small onion
4 beaten eggs
Dash pepper
3/4 lb. domestic Swiss cheese
   (1/2 grated - 1/2 cubed)
1/4 cup heavy cream
1/2 tsp. salt
Dash nutmeg

Combine grated cheese, flour, salt and pepper. Sauté onion. Add eggs and cheese cubes; cream and pour into unbaked pie shell. Dot with 1 tsp. butter; sprinkle with nutmeg.

Bake 30 to 35 minutes at 375°.

QUICHE LORRAINE

Crust
1 cup finely crushed cheese
   cracker crumbs (Ritz type)
1/4 cup melted butter
2 Tbs. poppy seed

Combine and press into 9 inch pie pan and bake at 350° for 8 minutes.

Filling
3 cups sliced onions
2 Tbs. butter
1 cup grated sharp Cheddar
   cheese
1/8 tsp. pepper
1 cup scalded milk
3 eggs, slightly beaten
1/2 tsp. salt

Sauté onions in butter until light yellow. Spoon over crust. Sprinkle on grated cheese. Combine scalded milk with beaten eggs and seasonings. Pour into crust.

Bake at 350° for 20 to 25 minutes or until knife inserted in center comes out clean. Garnish with parsley.

OVEN CHEESE FONDUE

10 slices white bread
6 eggs
3 cups milk
1 tsp. salt
2 Tbs. parsley
3 Tbs. chopped onion
2 cups shredded American
   cheese
1 tsp. dry mustard
1/2 cup chopped, cooked
   bacon

Heat oven to 325°. Remove crusts from bread. Cut into cubes. Beat eggs, milk and seasonings with beater. Stir into bread cubes. Add cheese, onions and bacon.

Pour into ungreased 11-1/2 x 7-1/2 x 1/2 inch baking dish. Bake uncovered for 1 hour or until center is set. Serve immediately.

Yield: 8 servings

CHEESE KNISHES

Use 1/2 of recipe for a yeast
   dough
1 lb. ground cottage cheese
1 egg
1 Tbs. sour cream
1 Tbs. vanilla
Dash of salt

Roll dough into rectangular shape. Spread with soft butter. Cut into squares. Fill with above mixture. Pinch edges together. Let rise until double in size. Bake 40 to 45 minutes at 350°. Serve with warm sour cream.

BLINTZES

1/2 cup water or milk
1/2 cup flour
1 egg

Mix egg and water or milk. Pour slowly into flour. Beat with fork. Let sit 5 minutes. Beat again.

Use a 7 inch skillet. Put in oil with paper towel. Let it get hot. Lower heat. Put batter in and out immediately. Hold over flame. When it curls around edge, take out shell.

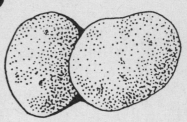

LYONNAISE POTATOES

1/4 cup vegetable oil
1 large onion, chopped
1-1/2 lbs. cold, boiled, peeled
 potatoes, cut into small,
 thick slices
1/2 cup chopped parsley
1/2 tsp. salt
1/2 tsp. pepper

Heat oil in large non-stick skillet. Add onion and potatoes and sauté over medium heat for about 20-25 minutes, until golden brown.
Remove from heat. Add parsley, salt and pepper. Mix well.

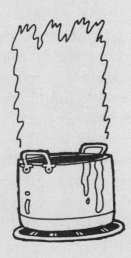

KNISHES

3 cups sifted all-purpose
 flour
1 tsp. baking powder
1/2 tsp. salt
1 cup water
1 egg, slightly beaten
Vegetable oil
Potato Filling
Kasha Filling
Chicken Liver Filling
Cheese Filling
1 egg yolk mixed with 1 Tbs.
 water

Measure flour, baking powder and salt into large bowl; add water, egg and 1 tablespoon oil. Stir with a wooden spoon until dough holds together; turn out onto lightly floured surface. Knead until smooth and elastic, using only enough extra flour to keep dough from sticking, about 5 minutes. Place dough on lightly floured surface; cover with bowl, let rest 30 minutes.

Divide dough into fourths. For each filling, roll out one fourth of dough on lightly floured surface to a 12-inch square; with a sharp knife, cut in half to make 2 six-inch wide strips. Brush lightly with oil. Spoon filling down center of each strip, dividing evenly.

Bring one side of pastry over filling, then roll up to enclose filling completely; pinch ends together. Put on lightly greased cookie sheet, seam side down.

Score with the blunt edge of a knife, at 1-inch intervals, do not cut through. Brush with egg yolk mixture. For Liver Knishes, cut each roll into 10 pieces. Pinch one end closed, pinch other end but leave a small opening. Place, closed side down on cookie sheet; brush tops with egg yolk mixture.

Bake in moderate oven (375°) 30 minutes, or until golden brown. Cut into 1-inch pieces for serving. Serve hot or warm.

Yield: 8 dozen appetizer knishes

Potato Filling
2 medium-size potatoes,
 cooked and mashed (1 cup)
2 Tbs. vegetable oil

3/4 cup finely chopped onion
3/4 tsp. salt
1/8 tsp. white pepper

Sauté onion in oil, stirring constantly, until tender but not brown, about 8 minutes.

Combine potatoes, onion, salt and pepper in small bowl. Mix well.

Yield: 1 cup or enough to fill 24 bite-size knishes

Kasha Filling
1/3 cup kasha
1-1/4 cups boiling water
3/4 tsp. salt
1/4 tsp. pepper
3/4 cup finely chopped onion
2 Tbs. vegetable oil

Heat kasha in a heavy medium-size saucepan, stirring constantly until toasted, about 5 minutes. Stir in water, salt and pepper. Cover; simmer 10 minutes, or until water is absorbed and kasha is just tender.

Sauté onion in oil, stirring often, until golden brown and tender about 10 minutes. Stir into kasha.
Yield: 1 cup or enough to fill 24 bite-size knishes

Chicken Liver Filling
l large onion, finely chopped
  (1 cup)
4 Tbs. vegetable oil
1/2 lb. chicken livers
1 tsp. salt
1/4 tsp. pepper

In a small skillet, sauté onion in 2 tablespoons of the oil, stirring often, until golden, about 10 minutes.

Remove onions to small bowl.

In same skillet, sauté chicken livers in remaining oil, stirring often, 5 minutes, or until livers have lost their pink color. Remove livers to a board and chop finely; add to onions in small bowl. Stir in salt and pepper.

Yield: 1 cup or enough to make 20 bite-size knishes.

Cheese Filling
1/2 cup pot cheese
3 or 4 oz. cream cheese
1 egg yolk
1 tsp. sugar
1/4 tsp. salt
1/4 tsp. vanilla

Combine pot cheese, cream cheese, egg yolk, sugar, salt and vanilla in a small bowl. Beat until well combined.

Yield: 1 cup or enough to fill 24 bite-size knishes

MOM SCHNEIDER'S COOKED POTATO DUMPLINGS (KLÖHSE)

8 potatoes
2 eggs, beaten
1 Tbs. salt
About 10 Tbs. flour (or
  enough to hold potatoes
  together)
1 onion

Boil potatoes with peels on. Chill. Peel and grate with onion. Add eggs, flour. (Can use ricer.) Shape into balls.

Boil 15 minutes in slow boiling salted water. Good with pork or beef roast.

POTATO DUMPLINGS II

8 to 10 cooked potatoes, cold
3 eggs
10 tbs. flour
1 tbs. salt
1 onion

Grind one onion when grinding the potatoes. Use meat grinder for cooked potatoes. Add a little butter. Form little balls, drop into boiling salted water and simmer for 20 minutes. Drain. Good with beef or pork roast.

POTATO PANCAKES (LATKES)

6 medium size potatoes
1 small onion (optional)
2 eggs, slightly beaten
3 Tbs. flour
1/4 tsp. pepper
1 tsp. salt
1/2 tsp. baking powder

Peel and grate potatoes and onion. Let stand 10 minutes so that liquid will rise to the top. Remove liquid. Stir in eggs. Add other ingredients. Drop by spoonfuls into a hot well-greased skillet. Brown on both sides. Drain on absorbent paper. Serve hot with applesauce, sugar or sour cream.

POTATO PANCAKES WITH CHEDDAR

1/2 cup grated cheddar
  cheese
1/3 cup milk
1 egg
1 small onion, grated
Applesauce
3 Tbs. flour
Shortening or salad oil
1/2 tsp. salt
4 medium potatoes

In a bowl, beat egg, then beat in milk, salt and flour. Add grated or chopped onion and grated cheese. Wash and peel potatoes, then grate directly into egg mixture, working rapidly because grated potato tends to darken.

In a heavy skillet, heat shortening or salad oil, using enough to coat surface generously. Add potato mixture by tablespoons and cook until brown and crisp on both sides. Serve hot with applesauce, as a main or side dish.

GOLDEN POTATO CASSEROLE

6 medium potatoes
1 pint dairy sour cream
10 oz. sharp cheddar, grated
1 bunch green onions, finely
  chopped
Boiling, salted water
1/4 cup milk
1 tsp. salt

2 Tbs. butter
1 cup soft bread crumbs

Scrub potatoes and cook covered in boiling, salted water until tender. Remove from water and cool. Peel potatoes and grate with coarse grater into a bowl.

Blend in sour cream, grated cheddar, chopped green onions, milk, salt and pepper. Mix well and transfer to a greased 9x13 inch pan or baking dish. Melt 2 tablespoons butter in small pan, add soft bread crumbs and mix well. Scatter over potato mixture.

Bake in preheated 300° oven for 50 minutes or until piping hot and golden brown. For a very crusty finish, bake extra 20 minutes. Cut into squares to serve.

Yield: 8 servings

BAKED POTATO STICKS

4 to 6 Idaho baking potatoes
2/3 cup butter, melted
2 Tbs. soy sauce
1/3 cup corn flake crumbs
1 Tbs. sesame seeds

Select 4 very large or 6 medium size baking potatoes. Scrub well and cut each potato into 6 or 8 wedges, lengthwise. Arrange on a baking sheet.

Combine melted butter and soy sauce and brush over potatoes. In small bowl, combine corn flake crumbs with sesame seeds. Sprinkle over potatoes. Bake in preheated 400° oven for 35 minutes or until crisp and lightly browned.

Yield: 6 servings

SAUTEED POTATOES

1 Tbs. vegetable oil
1 Tbs. butter
1/2 tsp. salt
1/4 tsp. pepper
1-1/2 lbs. (about 4 medium)
  all purpose potatoes, peeled
  and cut into 3/4 inch cubes

Drain potatoes on paper towels. In large heavy skillet, heat oil and butter until butter is melted. Add potatoes, turning to coat. Sauté over medium-high heat, shaking pan occasionally or tossing potatoes with spoon, for about 10 minutes or until potatoes begin to brown. Sprinkle with salt and pepper. Reduce heat to medium. Toss again. Cover skillet. Cook about 15 minutes more, shaking skillet or tossing occasionally until potatoes are golden and cooked through.

& RICES

CHEESY PASTA AND VEGETABLES

1 cup ricotta cheese
1/2 cup mozzarella cheese
1/2 cup grated Romano
  cheese
2 egg yolks
1 tsp. Italian seasoning,
  crumbled
1/8 tsp. garlic powder
Salt and pepper to taste
2 cups broccoli florets
1 cup chopped onion
3 medium carrots, sliced
2 celery stalks, sliced
1/2 lb. dried spaghetti
1 Tbs. vegetable oil
1 cup diced fresh tomatoes
1/2 cup chopped parsley

Combine cheese, egg yolks and seasonings in medium bowl. Set aside.

Steam broccoli, onions, carrots and celery until broccoli is crisp-tender, about 5 minutes.

Add spaghetti and oil to large pot of boiling water and cook until spaghetti is just tender but still firm to bite, about 5 minutes. Drain. Return to pot. Add steamed vegetables and toss. Add cheese mixture and toss. Transfer to serving bowl. Spoon tomatoes in center of pasta. Garnish with parsley.
Yield: 4 servings

BAKED ZITI WITH THREE CHEESES

1 pkg. (16 oz.) ziti
1 container (15 oz.) Ricotta
  cheese
1 pkg. (8 oz.) Mozzarella
  cheese, shredded
1 egg, lightly beaten
1/4 cup chopped parsley
1 garlic clove, minced
1/4 tsp. ground black pepper
Pinch ground nutmeg
1/4 cup grated Parmesan
  cheese

Cook pasta following package directions; drain.
Preheat oven to 350°. Grease 2-quart casserole. In large bowl, blend ricotta, 1 cup mozzarella, egg, parsley, garlic, pepper and nutmeg; stir in ziti. Spoon into prepared casserole and sprinkle with remaining mozzarella and Parmesan. Bake until top is golden, about 30 minutes.
Yield: 8 servings.

GARLIC & MUSHROOM PASTA

4 cups Marinara sauce
1 medium onion, chopped
1/2 lb. mushrooms, trimmed
  and chopped
2 heads oven-roasted garlic,
  squeeze from bulb
1 lb. pasta - linguine or
  spaghetti
1/2 tsp. ground black pepper
1/2 tsp. oregano
1/2 tsp. basil
1/2 tsp. parsley
1 to 2 Tbs. olive oil
Parmesan cheese, grated

Sauté the onion in 1 tablespoon olive oil, until soft and transparent. Add the mushrooms and continue cooking for 5 minutes. Add a little more oil, if necessary.

Add the onions, mushrooms and spices to the marinara sauce and simmer on low for 20 minutes. Add the garlic the last 5 minutes of cooking.

Cook pasta and drain. Top with sauce and dust with freshly grated Parmesan cheese.

SPINACH AND ARTICHOKE STUFFED SHELLS

1 (10 oz.) pkg. frozen
    chopped spinach, thawed
1 cup frozen artichoke hearts,
    thawed
12 jumbo pasta shells,
    uncooked
1 cup ricotta cheese
2 Tbs. basil
1 Tbs. fresh parsley, chopped
1/4 tsp. salt
2 Tbs. lemon juice
1/3 cup sour cream
2 Tbs. cornstarch
1-1/2 Tbs. basil
2 (14-1/2 oz.) cans tomatoes,
    undrained and chopped

Cook spinach and artichoke hearts as directed on package. Drain well. Chop artichoke hearts; set aside.

Cook pasta shells as directed. Drain and set aside. In a blender or food processor, add spinach, ricotta cheese, 2 tablespoons basil, parsley, salt and lemon juice. Blend or process until smooth. Transfer to a bowl and stir in the chopped artichoke and sour cream.

Combine tomato, cornstarch and 1-1/2 tablespoons basil in a sauce pan. Stir well and cook over medium heat until thickened.

Coat a 11x7x1-1/2 inch baking dish with vegetable spray. Spoon 1 cup tomato mixture into bottom of baking dish.

Spoon spinach mixture into shells. Arrange shells in baking dish. Pour remaining tomato mixture over shells. Bake uncovered at 350° for 30 minutes or until bubbly.

ZITI AND SPINACH BAKE

1 lb. zita
2/3 cup grated Parmesan
    cheese
3 large eggs, beaten
2 pkgs. (10 oz. each) frozen
    chopped spinach, thawed
    and drained well
1 container (15 oz.) Ricotta
    cheese
1/3 cup chopped fresh parsley
2 tsp. salt

2 tsp. pepper
1 jar (28 to 32 oz.) spaghetti
    sauce

Preheat oven to 375°. Cook ziti until just barely tender. Meanwhile, in a large bowl, combine all the rest of the ingredients and mix well.

Drain the ziti, toss it with the sauce and turn it into a greased 9x13 inch baking pan. Sprinkle 2 additional tablespoons of grated Parmesan cheese over the top and bake for 25 to 30 minutes, or until bubbly and lightly brown.

Yield: 4 to 6 servings
Note:
This is a simple recipe that tastes even better when made in advance.

LENTIL RICE QUICHE

2 cups cooked and cooled
    white rice
1 Tbs. margarine, melted
1 egg
1 cup grated Swiss cheese
1/2 cup sliced onions
1/2 cup fresh mushrooms
1/2 cup diced green pepper
1/2 cup fresh broccoli sprigs
1 cup cooked lentils
2 Tbs. chopped fresh parsley
2 eggs
3/4 cup milk
1/4 tsp. salt
1/8 tsp. pepper

In a medium sized bowl, combine cooked rice, melted margarine and slightly beaten egg. Pour into a buttered 9" pie plate, pressing against the sides and bottom to form a crust. Sprinkle 1/2 of the grated cheese on the bottom of the rice crust. Layer the vegetables and lentils on the cheese. Sprinkle the rest of the cheese over the vegetables. Sprinkle with chopped parsley.

Combine 2 eggs, milk, salt and pepper in a small bowl and carefully pour over the quiche filling.

Bake in a 400° oven for 30 minutes or until knife inserted 2" from the center returns clean. (Center should be very moist and not quite set when quiche is done. It will set up quickly.) Let quiche stand for 5 minutes before serving.

Yield: 6 servings

FETTUCINE ITALIANO

8 oz. fettucine
1/2 cup skim milk
1/3 cup mayonnaise, light
1 garlic clove, minced
1 egg, beaten
1/4 cup chopped parsley
5 crispy cooked bacon slices, crumbled
1/3 cup (1-1/2 oz.) grated Parmesan cheese

Prepare fettucine according to package directions. Drain. Gradually add milk to combined mayonnaise and garlic in small saucepan; heat thoroughly, stirring occasionally.

Remove from heat; blend in egg. Toss with hot fettucine until well-coated. Add remaining ingredients; toss lightly. Garnish with basil leaves, if desired. May substitute spaghetti for fettucine.

Yield: 5 servings

PASTA ITALIANO BAKE

1 lb. ground beef
1/4 cup chopped onion
1/4 cup chopped green pepper
1 garlic clove, minced
1 (6 oz.) can tomato paste
1/2 cup water
1 tsp. salt
1/2 tsp. oregano, crushed
1/4 cup parsley
2 eggs, beaten
2 cups (4 oz.) noodles, cooked, drained
1/2 cup mayonnaise
3/4 cup (3 oz.) grated Parmesan cheese

Brown meat; drain. Add onions, peppers and garlic; cook until tender. Stir in tomato paste, water and seasonings. Cover; simmer 15 minutes. Combine noodles and parsley; toss lightly. Combine mayonnaise, 1/2 cup cheese and eggs; mix well. Layer noodle mixture, mayonnaise mixture and meat mixture in 10x6 inch baking dish; top with remaining cheese. Bake at 350° for 25 minutes.

Yield: 6 servings

MEATLESS LASAGNA

Sauce
1 large onion, chopped
1 tsp. salt
1 garlic clove, minced
1/4 tsp. pepper
1 Tbs. oil
1 or 2 bay leaves
1 (28 oz.) can Italian tomatoes
1 tsp. oregano
1 (6 oz.) can tomato sauce
1 (4 oz.) can sliced mushrooms
1/2 cup water

Filling
1 container (24 oz.) cottage cheese
6 eggs
3/4 lb. grated Mozzarella cheese
6 to 8 lasagna noodles
Grated Parmesan cheese

Combine all sauce ingredients in a large pot. Simmer at least 1 hour. Cook noodles as directed on box. Beat eggs, mix in cottage cheese. Place sauce in bottom of large lasagna pan. Arrange layers of noodles, cheese, and sauce ending with sauce on top. Sprinkle with Parmesan cheese.

Bake 50 minutes at 375°. Let stand 10 minutes before serving.

Note:
This dish may be prepared in advance and frozen until ready to use. If freezing do not add Parmesan cheese, and do not bake.

NOODLE PUDDING DELUXE

Cook 1 lb. package of noodles and drain. Add:
6 eggs
1/2 lb. melted butter
l lb. Farmer's cheese
2 tsp. vanilla
1 pt. sour cream
1 tsp. salt
1/2 lb. cream cheese
2 cups milk
1/2 cup sugar

Mix all together. Put in well greased casserole pan. Sprinkle top with sugar and cinnamon. Bake for 1-1/4 hours at 350°.

SPAGHETTI CON LE VONGOLE (WITH CLAM SAUCE)

1/2 cup olive oil
1-1/2 tsp. minced garlic
1-1/2 cups clam broth
1/3 cup dry white wine
6-8 quarts of water
1-1/2 Tbs. salt
3 Tbs. soft butter
3 Tbs. fresh parsley, chopped
4 cans shucked, small clams
1-1/2 lbs. spaghetti or linguine
Salt and white pepper to taste

In a heavy 10 to 12 inch skillet, heat olive oil until a light haze forms over it. Stir in the garlic and cook over moderate heat, stirring constantly, for about 30 seconds. Pour over the clam broth and wine and boil briskly over high heat until the foam disappears and the liquid has reduced to about 1-1/4 cups. Remove from heat and set aside.

In a large kettle, bring water and salt to a bubbling boil over high heat. Drop the spaghetti in and stir gently with a wooden fork or spoon for a few moments to prevent the strands from sticking to one another   (Adding a couple of tablespoons of cooking oil to the boiling water will also help prevent sticking.) Boil over high heat, stirring occasionally, for about 7 to 12 minutes, or until the pasta is tender. Immediately drain the spaghetti into a colander, lifting the strands with a fork to be sure it is properly drained.   Transfer the spaghetti to a large heated serving bowl and toss it with the soft butter.

Bring the sauce in the skillet to a boil over high heat and add the clams. Heat the clams, turning them constantly, for 1 or 2 minutes. Then pour the clams and sauce over the spaghetti, sprinkle with parsley, and toss together with two large forks until all the ingredients are well mixed. Taste and season with white pepper. Serve at once.

Yield: 10 to 12 servings

13 SAUCES & TOPPINGS

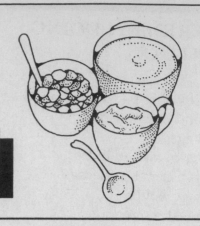

STONE CRAB'S MUSTARD SAUCE

3-1/2 tsp. Colman's dry
   English mustard
1 cup mayonnaise
2 tsp. Worcestershire sauce
1 tsp. A-1 sauce
2 Tbs. light cream
1/8 tsp. salt

Combine the mustard and mayonnaise in a bowl and beat for 1 minute. Add the remaining ingredients and beat until smooth and creamy. Serve as an accompaniment to fresh stone crab claws which have been cracked with a wide-headed mallet.
   Yield: 1-1/4 cups

AU POIVRE (PEPPERCORN SAUCE)

2 cups demi-glace
1-3/4 Tbs. freshly ground
   black pepper
1/2 Tbs. Dijon mustard
1/2 Tbs. sour cream
1 dash Tobasco

1/2 Tbs. whole green pepper-
   corns
1 Tbs. brandy
1 dash Worcestershire sauce

Simmer all ingredients together, add more pepper to taste. Serve over red meat or poultry.

BARBECUE SAUCE I

2 cups catsup
1 cup Worcestershire sauce
1 cup soy sauce
1 cup packed brown sugar
2 Tbs. liquid smoke
2 Tbs. tomato paste
2 cloves garlic, minced
Salt and pepper

Mix all ingredients until well blended. Place in refrigerator for two hours before using.

BECHAMEL SAUCE

1/8 lb. butter
1/2 cup flour
1-1/2 cup whole cream
Pinch of salt and pepper
1 pinch of granulated garlic
1/2 cup white wine

Using a sauce pan, melt the butter on medium heat. Add the flour slowly, continually stirring, making a roux. Cook the roux slowly for 5 minutes (don't scorch the flour). Add the cream and stir until the sauce is smooth. Add the salt, pepper, garlic and white wine. Stir and allow to cook 30 minutes on low heat.

BEARNAISE SAUCE

1/2 oz. fresh tarragon, chopped
2 oz. white wine
3 egg yolks
1 tsp. cool water
Dash of Tabasco
Dash of white pepper
1 tsp. lemon juice
1/4 tsp. Worcestershire sauce
3 oz. warm butter (120-140°)

Put tarragon and white wine in a small sauce pan and reduce over medium flame until wine is absorbed. Let cool. Over double boiler, whip egg yolks, water, Tabasco, white pepper, lemon juice and Worcestershire sauce until eggs start to thicken. Then slowly add butter. Remove bottom from the double boiler and fold in the tarragon reduction.

PESTO SAUCE

1 cup fresh basil leaves
1/2 tomato
2 garlic cloves
1/2 cup grated Parmesan cheese
1/2 cup pine nuts or walnuts
Salt and pepper to taste
1/4 cup olive oil
1 cup white wine
1/4 cup sliced mushrooms
1/4 cup heavy cream
1/8 cup whipped butter
Cooked fettucine or other pasta

Combine first 6 ingredients in food processor. Add olive oil slowly. Put in hot sauté pan, add wine and mushrooms, reduce for 20 seconds over high heat, then add cream and reduce another 20 seconds. Finish with butter and serve with fettucine or other pasta.

LENTIL SPAGHETTI SAUCE

2 Tbs. oil - vegetable or olive
1 medium onion, chopped
4 cloves garlic, minced
1 cup fresh mushrooms, sliced
8 oz. tomato sauce
4 oz. tomato paste
2-1/3 cups water
1/2 cups lentils, washed
1-1/2 tsp. crushed basil
1 tsp. dry oregano
1 tsp. white sugar
1 bay leaf
1/2 tsp. salt
1/8 tsp. pepper

Sauté onion, garlic and mushrooms in oil until onion is soft. Add remaining ingredients. Bring to boil. Reduce heat. Cover and let simmer on low heat for 30 to 40 minutes.
Yield: 6 servings

PICO DE GALLO

Dice one medium tomato, 1 whole jalapeno pepper and 1/2 avocado, peeled and seeded. Combine with 1/4 cup minced red onion, 1 Tbs. bottled teriyaki sauce, 2 tsp. lime juice and 1-1/2 tsp. minced fresh cilantro. Let stand at room temperature for 2 hours before serving so flavors can blend.

THAI TOMATO SALSA

2 green onions, cleaned, 3 inches green left on and slivered lengthwise
1/3 cup fresh lemon juice
1-1/2 large bunches cilantro, leaves removed and finely minced
2 cloves garlic, peeled and finely minced
1/4 cup slivered fresh basil leaves
4 ripe plum tomatoes, seeded and cut into 1/8 inch dice
1/4 cup peeled and diced purple onion (1/8 inch dice)
1-1/2 tsp. peeled and grated fresh ginger
1 Tbs. balsamic vinegar
1/4 to 1/3 cup olive oil
Salt and pepper to taste

In a small bowl, soak green onions in lemon juice for 30 minutes. Drain; reserve half of lemon juice. Mince green onions.
In a medium bowl, combine green onions, reserved lemon juice and remaining ingredients. Mix together well. Serve over grilled or broiled fish or chicken.
Yield: 6 to 8 servings

14 BREADS

TO BAKE

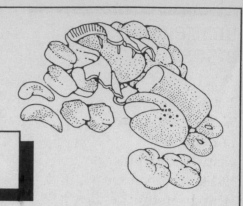

HINTS

Bread and rolls taste better and smell home-baked when heated just before serving. Warm in a 400° oven for 5-10 minutes, wrapped in tinfoil.

To freshen rolls, place in a paper bag, twist top of bag closed and heat in hot oven for 15 minutes.

Brown sugar kept in the bread box keeps bread moist and keeps brown sugar from hardening.

Instead of wrapping loaves of bread for freezing, package two to six slices, making it easier to defrost the amount of bread needed, leaving the rest of the loaf fresh.

Bread is less subject to mold if stored in the refrigerator, but turns stale more quickly.

If bread browns too quickly while baking, cover with brown paper for the last few minutes.

An ideal place to raise yeast dough is on top of the refrigerator; also near, but not on the range. Keep dough covered with a cloth to protect from drafts during rising.

Heat raisins in oven before adding to muffins or breads, and they will be more evenly distributed. Just wash them, then spread out on a flat pan. Cover and heat at 350° until they puff up.

To get the full flavor from raisins, cut them with scissors after heating.

Muffin tins may be lined with paper liners to avoid greasing of pans.

When scalding milk, first rinse saucepan with cold water, to prevent sticking. The top of a double boiler is an ideal place to heat milk without danger of boiling or scorching.

Yeast breads freeze extremely well. If glazing is desired, freeze them first, and when needed, heat and glaze.

Making yeast dough? You don't have to bake it all the same day. Place dough in the refrigerator once it is mixed. The top should be well-greased, then covered with wax paper, then a damp cloth. Be sure to keep the cloth damp. If made with milk and at least 1/4 cup sugar, it will keep about 3 days. If made with water, it will keep about 5 days. Cut off as much dough as you need at a time.

For a highly glazed crust on yeast breads, brush with beaten egg yolk before baking.

For a soft and tender crust, brush with soft butter or shortening while still warm. Cover with a towel to soften crust.

BUTTERMILK BISCUITS

2 cups all-purpose flour
5 Tbs. shortening
1/2 tsp. salt
4 tsp. baking powder
1/2 tsp. baking soda
1 cup buttermilk

Sift dry ingredients together. Cut in shortening. Add buttermilk all at once, stirring until dough follows fork around bowl. Turn out on floured board and knead for one minute. Pat out, not too thin, and cut with floured round cutter. Bake at 450° for 12 to 15 minutes.

SWEET POTATO MUFFINS

1-3/4 cups all-purpose flour
2 tsp. baking powder
1/4 tsp. salt
1/4 cup brown sugar, firmly
   packed
1 tsp. ground cinnamon
1/2 tsp. ground nutmeg
1/8 tsp. ground cloves
3/4 cup milk (whole or skim)
1/2 cup mashed, cooked
   sweet potato
3 Tbs. vegetable oil
1 egg, beaten lightly
1/2 tsp. vanilla
4 Tbs. raisins

Preheat oven to 400°. Coat muffin pan with non-stick vegetable spray.

Combine flour, baking powder, salt and brown sugar in a bowl. In another bowl, combine the rest of the ingredients, except the raisins. Add to dry ingredients, stirring just until moistened. Stir in raisins.

Spoon into prepared muffin pan, filling half full. Bake at 400° for 25 minutes, or until a toothpick inserted in center comes out clean.

Remove from pan immediately.

Yield: 1 dozen

ITALIAN HERB SPREAD

1 cup margarine, melted
1/3 cup Parmesan cheese
2 Tbs. Italian spice mix
1/2 tsp. garlic powder

Mix all ingredients together. Spread on French bread slices and broil.

GARLIC ONION SPREAD

1/2 cup margarine, melted
1/4 cup green onion, thinly sliced
1 clove garlic, minced

Mix all ingredients together and spread on French bread slices and bake or broil.

FORGOZA BREAD

12 oz. white bread dough
   (frozen loaf may be used)
1/4 cup sliced fresh scallions
1/4 cup chopped fresh parsley
3 Tbs. fresh garlic, minced
1/4 cup Parmesan cheese
1 tsp. oregano
1 cup shredded sharp
   Cheddar cheese
6 Tbs. olive oil

On an unfloured surface, roll the bread dough out to 1 inch thickness. Sprinkle the scallions, parsley, garlic, Parmesan cheese, oregano and cheddar cheese on top of dough. Finally, drizzle the olive oil over all the ingredients.

Roll the dough up as you would a jelly roll. Using a sharp knife, chop the dough into medium-size pieces. Heap into a 9 inch pan. Cover with a damp cloth and allow to rise until doubled in size (about 45 minutes depending upon the dough and the weather conditions).

Bake in preheated 400° oven about 25 minutes or until center is fully baked and bread is golden. Serve warm.

ENGLISH MUFFINS

1 pkg. yeast
1/4 cup warm water
1-1/4 cup scalded milk
2 Tbs. sugar
1 tsp. salt
1/4 cup butter
3 cups sifted flour
1 cup corn meal

Soften yeast in warm water. Pour scalded milk over sugar, salt and butter; cool to lukewarm.

Stir in 1 cup flour; add softened yeast and corn meal, mixing well. Beat 2 minutes at medium speed on electric mixer. Beat in remaining flour to make soft dough.

Cover and let rise in warm place until double in bulk—about 1 hour. Stir down dough. Roll out to about 1 inch on surface sprinkled heavily with corn meal. Cut with 3 inch round cutter. Cover and let rest for 30 minutes.

Preheat griddle to medium hot. Grease griddle lightly. Carefully place muffins, corn meal side down, on griddle.

Bake until bottom is nicely brown—-about 20 minutes. Turn and bake an additional 20 minutes.

Store in refrigerator until time to serve. Then split with fork and toast under broiler.

BREAD

1 pkg. yeast
2 cups scalded milk
2 Tbs. sugar
2 tsp. salt
1 Tbs. shortening
6-to 6-1/4 cups sifted flour

Soften yeast in warm water.
Combine hot milk, sugar, salt and shortening. Cool to lukewarm. Stir in 2 cups flour and beat well. Add yeast and mix again. Now add just enough of remaining flour to make a moderately stiff dough.

Turn dough out on lightly floured surface and knead until smooth and satiny (about 8 to 10 minutes). Form in ball and place in slightly greased bowl, turning to grease surface. Cover and let sit in warm place until double in bulk (about 1-1/2 hours).

Punch down and let rise again until double in bulk (about 45 minutes). Divide in half. Shape each piece of dough in smooth ball. Cover; let rest for 10 minutes.

Shape in loaves and place in 2 greased 8-1/2x4-1/2x2-1/2 inch loaf pans. Let rise for about 1 hour.

Bake for 35 minutes at 400° until brown. If tops are browning too rapidly after 15 minutes, cover with foil. Remove from pans and cool on racks.

MEXICAN FRIED BREAD

4 cups sifted flour
1 tsp. salt
2 Tbs. vegetable shortening
3 Tbs. baking powder
2 Tbs. sugar
1 cup milk
Vegetable oil for frying

Sift flour, baking powder, salt and sugar into a large bowl. Cut in shortening until mixture resembles cornmeal. Stir in milk until mixture forms a firm dough.

Knead dough on a lightly floured surface just until smooth. Cover, let rest for 20 minutes. Roll out to 1/4 inch thickness; cut into squares or diamonds.

Heat oil in a deep saucepan or deep fat fryer to 375° on deep fat frying thermometer. Fry dough a few at a time, turning often so they fry evenly, until golden brown. Remove from oil with slotted spoon onto paper towel to drain. Serve hot with butter (with a meal) or sprinkled with cinnamon-sugar or with a pitcher of warm honey (for dessert).

CASSEROLE BREAD

1 cup milk
1 cup warm water
3 Tbs. sugar
2 pkgs. yeast
2 tsp. salt
1/2 tsp. garlic powder
2 Tbs. butter
4 cups unsifted flour

Scald milk; stir in sugar, salt and butter; cool to lukewarm.

Measure warm water into large warm bowl. Sprinkle in yeast; stir until dissolved. Stir in lukewarm milk mixture. Add garlic powder and flour; stir to blend, then beat until well blended, about 2 minutes. Cover; let rise in warm place, free from draft for about 40 minutes or until doubled in bulk.

Stir down. Beat vigorously about 1/2 minute. Turn into greased 1-1/2 quart casserole, or greased 9 inch tube pan. Bake immediately in moderate over at 375° for about 1 hour.
Serve warm with melted butter.

BRIOCHE

1 pkg. active dry yeast
1/4 cup warm water
1/2 cup milk
1/2 cup butter
1/3 cup sugar
1/2 tsp. salt
3-1/4 cup flour
3 eggs, beaten
1 egg yolk, beaten (save egg white to combine with 1 Tbs. sugar later)

Soften active dry yeast in warm water.

Scald milk and cool to lukewarm.

Cream butter, sugar and salt until fluffy. Add milk. Add 1 cup flour. Add softened yeast, eggs and egg yolk, beating well. Add remaining flour and beat 5 to 8 minutes longer.

Cover and let double in bulk (about 2 hours). Stir down and beat well. Cover with foil and refrigerate overnight. Stir down; turn out on lightly floured surface. Divide dough in fourths, set aside 1/4 of dough.

Cut remaining 3 pieces in half and form each piece into 4 balls. Place balls of dough in muffin pans. With thumb, poke indention in top of each ball-brushing holes slightly with water.

Cut reserved dough into 4 wedges; divide each into 6 pieces and shape into 24 small balls. Press small ball in the indention of each large ball of dough.
Cover and let rise about 1 hour.

Combine slightly beaten egg white and 1 Tbs. sugar; brush on brioche.

Bake in moderate oven at 375° for 15 minutes, or until done.

CHALLAH #1

1 pkg. yeast
1/4 cup warm water
2 tsp. sugar
4-1/2 cups sifted flour
1 cup warm water
2 tsp. salt
1/8 tsp. saffron
2 eggs
2 Tbs. vegetable oil
1 egg yolk, slightly beaten

Sprinkle yeast on 1/4 cup warm water; stir to dissolve. Add sugar; mix well; let stand 5 minutes.

Sift flour with salt and saffron. Make a "well" in center; drop in 2 eggs, oil, warm water and yeast mixture; work into flour.

Knead on floured surface until smooth and elastic. Shape into a ball; place in greased bowl; turn over to bring greased surface to top. Cover; set in warm place free from draft; let rise 1 hour. Punch down; cover; let rise until double in size.

Divide dough into 3 equal portions. With floured hands, roll each portion into 3 strips of equal lengths. Braid strips together; seal ends. Place in bread pan; cover, let rise again until double in size. Brush with egg yolk.
Bake at 350° about 50 minutes or until golden brown.

15 DESSERTS

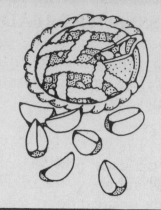

& PIES

HINTS

To prevent juices from leaking out of pies, wrap wet pastry tape around edge of pie, or insert 1-1/2 inch pieces of uncooked macaroni in several of the slits in the top of the pie.

Sprinkle fine bread crumbs on the bottom crust to avoid leaking from fruit pies.

Do not over handle pie dough as it tends to toughen.

If you have leftover pastry, roll it very thin, place in muffin tins, fill with 1 tsp. jam and garnish with coconut. Bake at 350 for 10 to 12 minutes.

Cut leftover pastry in fancy shapes, bake and decorate smooth topped pies.

For a flaky top for your pies, brush top crust with a little water.

For a sugary top, remove pie from oven 5 minutes before done, sprinkle with sugar and return to oven.

An 8 inch pie makes approximately 6 servings, and a 9 inch pie makes about 8 servings.

Baked crusts should be cooled before pouring in the filling.

Always seal meringue to edges of pie to prevent shrinkage.

Sprinkle a little granulated sugar over meringue before browning to produce a topping that will cut more easily.

To fill cream puffs, make a small opening in the top of the puff, put filling into a pastry tube, insert nozzle of tube into opening and squeeze to fill.

When making jello molds, first grease mold lightly to prevent sticking when unmolding. Dip pan quickly into hot water, count to 3 and invert onto serving plate. Another way is to invert mold on plate and cover with a hot towel for a few minutes.

Sprinkle banana slices with lemon juice to prevent discoloration.

Drain juice from canned fruits and rinse well with cold water. Washes away those unneeded calories.

Heat canned cherry pie filling and add a little water. It makes a sauce consistency. Stir in brandy to taste. Molds or desserts are delicious with this topping.

Coarsely crumbled macaroons or sugar-coated cereals make extra good toppings for individual servings of dessert.

For an easy parfait, fill tall glasses with alternate layers of prepared chocolate pudding and marshmallow topping or sweetened whipped cream.

If you are baking apples, first prick their skins. They will not burst during baking.

One package of dessert topping or 1/2 pint whipping cream yields 2 cups when whipped. They may be used interchangeably.

For best results when whipping cream, first chill bowl and beaters.

Do not overbeat whipping cream or it will turn to butter.

Store ice cream at zero temperature. Remove from freezer and let stand just until able to remove from container. Close securely before replacing in the freezer.

Use a dry ice cream scoop, or drops of water will remain on the ice cream, which will form ice crystals when frozen.

GENERAL INSTRUCTIONS FOR PERFECT PASTRY

Roll out dough about 1/8 inch thick. Board should be lightly floured and the rolling pin should have a stocking cover or be lightly floured.

Keep pastry circular and roll it 1 inch larger than inverted pie plate.

Fold in half and transfer to pie plate.

Unfold, being careful not to stretch dough.

Fill as desired, and trim off overhanging edges.

Roll out the top crust, keeping pastry circular and 1 inch larger than the pie plate.

Fold in half and make several slits to allow steam to escape.

Moisten edge of bottom pastry with water.

Place top crust over filling and unfold.

Fold the overlapping edge of the top crust under the edge of the lower crust. Seal thoroughly.

Flute edges, or press with the tines of a fork, making sure that edges are hooked on to the rim of the pie plate.

Cover edges with a strip of tinfoil to prevent overbrowning. Remove foil 15 minutes before end of baking time. Bake as directed.

HOMEMADE

DESSERTS

FRUIT AMBROSIA

1 (20 oz.) can fruit cocktail, drained (reserve syrup)
1 (11 oz.) can mandarin oranges, drained (reserve syrup)
1 (6 oz.) or 2 (3 oz.) package vanilla instant pudding mix
1 cup shredded coconut
1 cup miniature marshmallows
1 cup frozen dessert topping, thawed
1 cup sour cream

Whip instant pudding mix with reserved fruit syrups until well blended. Add drained fruits, coconut and marshmallows. Stir to mix well. Fold in gently the sour cream and whipped topping. Chill until serving time, at least two hours, but overnight is better.
Yield: 8 to 10 servings

CONGEALED HEAVENLY HASH

1 (15-1/2 oz.,) can pineapple chunks, drained (reserve syrup)
1-3/4 cups liquid (reserved syrup plus water)
1 (3 oz.) pkg. lemon gelatin
1 cup whipping cream, whipped or 1 pkg. dessert topping mix, prepared according to directions
4 cups miniature marshmallows
1-1/4 cups halved grapes

2 oranges, cut up or 1 (11 oz.) can mandarin oranges, drained

In small saucepan, heat 1 cup liquid to boiling. In large bowl, add boiling liquid to gelatin; stir to dissolve. Add remaining liquid and chill until thickened, but not set. Fold in whipped cream (or prepared dessert topping). Add remaining ingredients; blend well. Cover and refrigerate several hours or overnight. Will keep for 2 days when dessert topping is used.
Yield: 8 servings

FLAN I

Caramel
3/4 cup sugar
2 tablespoons water

Cook white sugar in a skillet over medium heat, stirring constantly, until the sugar forms a golden brown syrup. Immediately pour caramel into 9 inch round cake pan, swirling to coat bottom. (Do not use pan with removable bottom.) Place cake pan in roasting pan; set aside.

4 cups milk
1 vanilla bean or 1 Tbs. vanilla extract
2 strips (3 inches each) orange peel
1 cinnamon stick
6 large eggs
2/3 cup sugar

Preheat oven to 300°. Heat milk in sauce pan to simmer. Split vanilla bean lengthwise and scrape out seeds; add bean and seeds, orange peel and cinnamon to milk. Cover and let stand 10 minutes. Return milk mixture to boil.
Lightly beat eggs and sugar with vanilla extract, if using, in bowl. Gradually whisk hot milk into eggs. Strain custard through fine sieve into cake pan, discarding vanilla bean, peel and cinnamon. Place pans in oven. Pour enough boiling water into roasting pan to come halfway up side of cake pan.
Bake 45 to 50 minutes, until knife inserted 2 inches from edge comes out clean. Let stand in water bath 10 minutes. Cool. Cover and refrigerate up to 24 hours. Cut around edge and invert onto large serving plate.
Yield: 8 servings

BLUEBERRY CREAM PIE

1 baked 9 inch pie shell
1 (3 oz.) pkg. strawberry gelatin
1-1/4 cups boiling water
1 pint vanilla ice cream
2 cups fresh or frozen blueberries, rinsed and drained
1 cup heavy cream, whipped
1/4 cups confectioner's sugar
1 tsp. vanilla extract

Cool pie shell.
Dissolve gelatin in boiling water. Cut ice cream into

cubes and drop cubes into hot gelatin, one at a time, stirring until ice cream is melted. Chill until slightly thickened.

Fold in 1-1/2 cups of the blueberries. Pour filling into pie shell. Chill until firm.

Whip cream with sugar and vanilla. Put cream into a pastry bag and pipe with a rosette tip into a lattice on top of pie. Fill lattice with remaining blueberries. Chill until ready to serve.

Yield: one 9 inch pie

PINEAPPLE CREAM PUFFS

8 baked Cream Puff Shells
1 (3-1/4 oz.) pkg. vanilla
   pudding mix (not instant)
1-1/4 cups milk
1-1/2 tsp. grated orange peel
1 tsp. vanilla extract
1/4 tsp. almond extract
1/8 tsp. salt
1 (1 lb.-4 oz.) can pineapple
   chunks
1 cup whipping cream
Powdered sugar

Bake and cool Cream Puff Shells. Turn pudding mix into small saucepan and blend in milk. Cook over moderate heat, stirring constantly, until pudding just reaches a boil. Remove from heat, and stir in orange peel, vanilla and almond extracts and salt. Cool, stirring now and then, to avoid crust forming on top.

Drain pineapple well. Beat cream until stiff. Fold into

cooled pudding. Fold in pineapple chunks. Refrigerate. Shortly before serving, cut puffs in halves, and pull out any soft strands inside. Fill with the pineapple cream mixture.

Yield: 8 servings

Cream Puff Shells
3/4 cup water
6 Tbs. butter or margarine
1/4 tsp. salt
3/4 cup sifted all-purpose
   flour
3 large eggs

Heat water, butter and salt to boiling. Add flour all at once. Cook, stirring constantly, until mixture is very thick, and forms a ball that follows spoon around. Remove from heat. Add eggs, one at a time, beating well after each addition. Beat until dough is smooth and shiny. Spoon in 8 high mounds on lightly greased baking sheet. Bake in hot oven (400°) about 40 minutes until well puffed and golden brown. Remove to wire rack to cool.

Yield: 8 shells

NO-DOUGH BLUEBERRY-PEACH COBBLER

1/2 cup butter or margarine
1 cup all-purpose flour
3/4 cup sugar
2 tsp. baking powder
1/2 cup milk
2 cups fresh sliced peaches

2 cups fresh blueberries
1/2 cup sugar

Melt butter in a 2-1/2 quart baking dish. Set aside. Combine flour, 3/4 cup sugar, and baking powder; add milk, and stir until blended. Pour batter over butter in baking dish; do not stir.

Combine peaches, blueberries, and 1/2 cup sugar; spoon over batter. do not stir. Bake at 350° for 45 to 55 minutes.

Yield: 6 servings

CHERRY COBBLER

2 (1 lb. 5 oz. each) cans cherry
   pie filling
1-1/2 cups sifted all-purpose
   flour
2 tsp. baking powder
1/4 cup sugar
1/2 tsp. salt
1/4 cup (1/2 stick) butter
1/2 cup milk
1/2 cup toasted slivered
   almonds
2 Tbs. sugar
Light cream or half-and-half

Preheat oven to hot (400°). Spoon cherry pie filling into a shallow 3-quart baking dish.

Sift flour, baking powder, the 1/4 cup sugar and salt into a bowl; cut in butter with pastry blender until mixture is crumbly. Stir in milk until a stiff dough forms. Drop by tablespoonful onto cherries. Sprinkle with toasted almonds and sugar.

Bake for 30 minutes or until topping is golden brown. Serve warm with cream.

Yield: 8 servings

BLACKBERRY COBBLER

1 cup self-rising flour
1 cup water
2 cups blackberries
1 cup sugar
1 stick margarine

Combine flour, sugar and water.

Pour batter into baking dish and place fresh fruit or berries on top, then drizzle melted margarine over the fruit.

Bake at 350° for about 30 minutes. Batter rises on top and makes a nice topping for cobbler.

Serve warm with cream poured over top or with ice-cream or whipped cream. Fruit and berry cobbler can also be made by using seasonal fruit and sugar to taste, depending on the tartness of the fruit. Quick-cooking tapioca is a good thickening agent. Use 2 tablespoons for a 9 inch pie, more if using a juicy berry. Flour and corn-starch also can be used as thickening agents.

TIRA MISU

8 oz. cream cheese, cut into pieces, room temperature
1 cup sugar
1-1/2 tsp. vanilla

2 Tbs. milk
2 Tbs. brandy
1-3/4 cups heavy cream, chilled
1-1/4 cups Espresso, fresh
1 (7 oz.) pkg. Ladyfingers
1/4 cup cocoa powder

Beat cream cheese, sugar and milk until the mixture is smooth and fluffy. Blend in vanilla and brandy. Transfer to a medium bowl.

Whip heavy cream until stiff and fold into the cream cheese mixture. Cover and refrigerate until well chilled, at least 1 hour. (This can be prepared 2 days ahead.)

Pour coffee into a large shallow dish. Dip the Ladyfingers in the coffee, turning to coat all sides. Do not saturate.

Arrange Ladyfingers in a 9-1/2x12-1/2x2 inch serving dish. Pour in the cream cheese mixture and smooth the top.

Put cocoa in a small sieve and dust the top of the dessert evenly. Refrigerate.

Yield: 8 servings

STRAWBERRY YOGURT TRIFLE

4 cups whole strawberries
2 tsp. sugar
5 Tbs. orange juice
6 slices (1/2 inch thick) Angel Food Cake
1-1/2 (8 oz.) carton of straw-berry low fat yogurt

Wash and hull strawberries.

Reserve 4 or 5 for garnish. Thinly slice remaining strawberries and toss with sugar and orange juice.

Line the bottom of a deep-sided, clear glass 1-1/2 quart dish with 3 slices of the cake, piecing, if needed. Spoon 1/2 of the strawberry and juice mixture over the cake, then top with 1/2 of the yogurt. Repeat second layer with the remaining cake, berries and yogurt. Garnish with whole berries. Chill well before serving.

Best when refrigerated overnight.

Note:
If desired, recipe may be assembled in small individual glass dishes.

BANANA YOGURT TRIFLE

1-1/2 cups thinly sliced bananas
1/3 cup orange juice
6 slices Angel Food Cake (1/2 inch thick)
1-1/2 (8 oz.) strawberry/banana low-fat yogurt

In a bowl, gently toss bananas with the orange juice. Layer one-sided clear glass 1 quart dish with 3 slices of the cake. Layer with fruit and yogurt. Repeat layering.

Yield: 4 to 6 servings

PEACH YOGURT TRIFLE

2 cups fresh peaches, thinly
   sliced
2 tsp. sugar
3 or 4 Tbs. orange juice
8 slices Angel Food Cake
   (1/2 inch thick)
2 tsp. peach-flavored
   Schnapps (optional)
1-1/2 (8 oz.) carton peach
   low-fat yogurt

Toss peaches with sugar and orange juice. Layer deep-sided clear glass 1 quart dish with 3 slices of the cake. Drizzle with Schnapps. Layer with fruit and yogurt. Repeat layering.
   Yield: 4 to 6 servings

BAKLAVA

2 cups chopped or ground
   walnuts
1/2 tsp. cinnamon
1 lb. filo sheets
1 cup butter or margarine,
   melted

Combine nuts and cinnamon. Butter the bottom of a 13x9 inch baking pan. Lay 7 filo sheets in pan, brushing each sheet with melted butter. Sprinkle 1/2 of the nut mixture over filo. Drizzle with melted butter. Top with 7 more filo sheets, brushing each with butter. Sprinkle with the other half of nut mixture and drizzle with butter. Top with remaining filo, again brushing each with melted butter. Cut top layer only into diamond shaped pieces. Bake in preheated oven at 350° for 1 hour.

Syrup
2 cups sugar
1 tsp. lemon juice
1-1/2 cups water
1/2 cup honey

Combine sugar, water and lemon juice in saucepan and boil 15 minutes. Stir in honey.
   When baklava comes from oven, cut through bottom layer. Cook 10 minutes. Pour warm syrup over.

CHOCOLATE COCONUT CHIFFON RING

1 envelope unflavored gelatin
1-1/2 cups cold milk
2/3 cups sugar
1/4 tsp. salt
1 sq. unsweetened chocolate
3 egg yolks, slightly beaten
3 egg whites, stiffly beaten
1 tsp. vanilla
1 small pkg. Baker's coconut
1/2 cup chilled heavy cream,
   whipped
3 Tsp. Baker's 4 in 1 cocoa
   mix

Soften gelatin in milk. Add 1/3 cup of the sugar, salt and chocolate. Cook over hot water until chocolate is thoroughly dissolved. Beat with rotary beater until well blended. Pour slowly over egg yolks. Cook and stir 3 minutes longer. Cool 10 minutes. Add remaining 1/3 cup sugar to beaten egg whites, beat to stiff peaks. Blend in chocolate mixture. Add vanilla and half of the coconut. Turn into 1 quart ring mold. Chill until very firm. Unmold.
   Whip the heavy cream, adding the 4 in 1 cocoa mix. Spread whip cream mixture over mold. Top with remaining coconut.
   Yield: 8 servings

CHOCOLATE ON CHOCOLATE PIE

1 cup sugar
1 stick (8 Tbs.) unsalted butter or margarine
1/2 cup cornstarch
2 large eggs
1 pkg. (6 oz.) semi-sweet
   chocolate chips
1 cup chopped pecans
1 unbaked 9 inch pie shell

Preheat oven to 350°. Combine sugar, butter, cornstarch, eggs and vanilla extract in a large bowl; mix well. Stir in chocolate chips and pecans. Pour mixture into pie shell. Bake until the filling begins to pull away from the sides of the crust, about 40 minutes.
   Cool completely on rack. Serve with a dollop of whipped cream and a drizzle of chocolate syrup, if desired.

SOUR CREAM PIE

1 cup sour cream
1 pkg. (8 oz.) cream cheese, softened
1/3 cup granulated sugar
2 tsp. vanilla
1 (8 oz.) container whipped topping, thawed
1 prepared 9 inch graham cracker pie crust

Combine sour cream, cream cheese, sugar and vanilla in large bowl; mix well. Fold in whipped topping; then pour into the pie crust. Chill for at least 2 hours before serving.
Yield: 8 servings

TRES LECHES

1 (14 oz.) can sweetened condensed milk
1 (12 oz.) can evaporated milk
1 pint half-and half
Pinch of salt
2 prepared pound cakes (12 oz. each)
1 (8 oz.) container frozen whipped topping, thawed

Combine sweetened condensed milk, evaporated milk, half-and-half and salt in a large bowl; stir well and set aside. Cut pound cakes into six-inch slices each. Lay slices tightly into the bottom of a 9x13 inch baking dish or pan. Pour milk mixture evenly over the cake slices, cover and refrigerate for about 2 or 3 hours. Remove cake from refrigerator and spread whipped topping over the cake. Chill for an additional 1 to 2 hours, then garnish with fresh berries, other fresh fruit or your favorite pie filling before serving.
Yield: 12 to 15 servings

SINGLE PIE CRUST

1 cup sifted flour
1/3 cup shortening
3 Tbs. cold water, brimming
1/2 tsp. salt

With pastry blender, chop flour, shortening and salt until about the size of peas. Add water and cut with blender until no dry flour remains. Press together in wax paper and roll on well-floured pastry cloth.
Fit into pie pan, allowing about 1 inch to protrude over edge. Bake in 450° oven for 10 minutes, then reduce heat to 325° and finish.

DOUBLE PIE CRUST

1-1/2 cups flour
1/2 tsp. salt
1/2 cup shortening
4 Tbs. cold water

Shortening produces a flakier and whiter crust. Sift dry ingredients together, cut into shortening with blender, or two knives, adding water gradually. To eliminate handling with bare hands, turn out onto heavy wax paper and press firmly together until a smooth mass; divide in half for bottom and upper crusts.
Toss half on pastry cloth and roll lightly until about 1/4 inch thick. To insure extra flakiness, fold each end toward center, then fold across in half and now roll to 1/8 inch thickness.
Fit into pie tin, allowing about 1 inch to project over edge, use desired filling, roll out dough for upper crust; pierce about 6 holes for air vents; fit over pie and crimp; seal edge.
Bake in 450° oven for 10 minutes, reducing to about 325° until finished.

APPLE PIE

Apples
1/4 tsp. salt
1 cup sugar
2 Tbs. lemon juice
Rind of lemon
1/2 tsp. cinnamon
1/4 tsp. nutmeg
Butter

Slice enough apples to fill pan. Add sugar, salt, lemon juice, rind of lemon, cinnamon and nutmeg; mix well and put into unbaked shell. Dot generously with butter. Cover with top crust and bake on center shelf of 450° oven for 10 minutes. Reduce heat to 350° and continue baking for about 30 minutes.

FANNY'S PIE CRUST

3/4 cup Crisco
2 cups flour
1/4 cup hot water
1 Tbs. milk

Mix all ingredients. Roll.
Yield: 2 (8 inch) pie crusts

LIME CHIFFON PIE

1 envelope unflavored gelatin
1/2 cup cold water
1 tsp. grated lemon peel
3 eggs, separated
1 (9 inch) baked pie crust
1/2 cup lime juice
1 cup whipped cream
1/4 tsp. salt
1 cup sugar, divided
Green food coloring

Soften gelatin in cold water. In top of double boiler, beat egg yolks slightly; add 2/3 cup sugar, lime juice and salt. Cook over hot water until thick, stirring constantly; remove from heat. Stir in softened gelatin until thoroughly dissolved. Tint with food coloring until pale green. Chill until slightly thickened. Beat egg whites until stiff - not dry. Gradually beat in remaining 1/3 cup sugar and grated peel. Fold in gelatin mixture. Then fold in half of the whipped cream. Pile into cooled pie shell. Chill until firm. Swirl remaining whipped cream onto top of pie. Refrigerate until served.

DEATH BY CHOCOLATE

1 (19.8 oz.) family size fudge brownie mix
1/4 to 1/2 cup Kahlua or coffee liqueur
3 (3.5 oz. each) boxes Jello chocolate mousse
8 (1.2 to 1.4 oz. size) Skor or Heath candy bars
1 (12 oz.) container whipped topping

Bake brownies according to package directions; cool. Punch holes in brownies with fork; pour Kahlua over brownies and set aside. Make Jello chocolate mousse according to package directions. Break Skor or Heath bars into small pieces in food processor or by tapping them with a hammer (right in the wrapper).

Crumble half of the soaked brownies and place in the bottom of a glass trifle dish. Cover with half of the mousse, layer with half the candy and then add half of the whipped topping. Repeat layers with the remaining ingredients.

Instead of the alcohol, you may substitute a mixture of 1 tsp. sugar and 4 Tbs. left over black coffee.

FLAN II

1 can Eagle Brand sweetened condensed milk
5 eggs
1 tsp. vanilla
2 cups hot water
1/2 cup sugar

In Bundt pan, melt 1/2 cup sugar until brown. Coat pan and let stand.

In electric mixer's large bowl, put milk, 2 cups hot water, vanilla and eggs. Beat until fluffy.

Pour mixture into Bundt pan over caramelized sugar.

Place in a pan of water in oven at 475° for 30 minutes. After 15 minutes, slide a piece of aluminum foil over top of pan so Flan won't be too brown.

Allow to cool completely. Run knife around Flan and turn out onto platter. Carmelized sugar will flow over top and sides. Keep refrigerated.

FUDGE PECAN PIE

1 cup granulated or brown sugar
3 eggs
3/4 cup cocoa powder
1/4 tsp. salt
3/4 cup corn syrup
1/4 cup melted butter
1-1/2 cups pecans
1 Tbs. brandy
1 tsp. vanilla
1 (9 inch) unbaked pie shell

Beat eggs in large bowl. In another bowl, blend sugar, cocoa, and salt until smooth. Gradually beat cocoa mixture into eggs, then add syrup, butter, pecans, brandy and vanilla; mix well.

Pour into pie shell and bake in 325° oven for about 1 hour, or until filling rises up and sets. Toothpick should come out clean when inserted near center. Let cool and serve.

Yield: 8 servings

SIMPLE PECAN PIE

1 cup sugar
6 tsp. melted butter
3 eggs, beaten
1/2 cup dark corn syrup
1 tsp. vanilla
1 cup pecans

Beat eggs thoroughly with sugar, corn syrup, melted butter and vanilla. Add pecans. Pour into unbaked 9 inch pie shell. Bake at 350° for 45 minutes to 1 hour, or until knife inserted halfway between outside and center comes out clean.

PECAN PIE

1 cup sugar
3/4 cup light Karo syrup
2 Tbs. flour
3 eggs
1 cup pecans
Small amount butter
1 tsp. vanilla
Frozen pie shell, thawed

Mix the above ingredients

and put in pie shell. Bake 45 minutes to 1 hour at 350°.

TUTTI-FRUTTI TORTONI

1 pint vanilla ice cream, softened
1/2 cup crumbled macaroons
1/3 cup peach flavored brandy
1/3 cup chopped toasted pecans
1 can (16 or 17 oz.) fruit cocktail, well drained

Line 12 cup muffin pan with paper liners; set aside. In large bowl, combine all ingredients. Stir until well blended. Spoon evenly into paper liners. Cover with plastic wrap. Freeze 3 hours.

Note:
This dessert is a breeze. Can be made ahead and frozen.

PLUM WHIP 3 EGG WHITES

1/4 tsp. salt
1 (16 or 17 oz.) can purple plums, drained, pitted and finely chopped
1/4 cup finely chopped pecans
1/3 cup sugar
1/2 tsp. grated lemon peel

Preheat oven to 350°. In large mixing bowl, beat egg whites and salt until foamy. Continue beating, adding

sugar a tablespoon at a time until stiff. Fold in plums, pecans and lemon peel. Spoon into 1-1/2 quart casserole. Place casserole in larger baking pan. Fill pan with 1-1/2 to 2 inches hot water. Bake 30 to 35 minutes until golden and spongy. Serve warm with custard sauce.

Custard Sauce
1 cup milk
3 egg yolks
2 Tbs. sugar
1 tsp. cornstarch
1 tsp. vanilla extract

In small saucepan, heat milk until bubbles form around the edge of the pan. Meanwhile, in a small bowl, beat egg yolks, sugar and cornstarch until smooth. Add milk gradually and stir until smooth. Return mixture to pan; cook over medium heat, stirring constantly just until mixture comes to a boil. Cool sauce slightly, stir in vanilla.

PEACH SMOOTHIE

Cut a 3 oz. pkg. cream cheese into chunks and put into blender container.

Drain a 16 oz. can of peaches in heavy syrup, reserving 3 Tbs. syrup. Blend fruit, syrup, 1 Tbs. dark rum until smooth.

Stir in an 8 oz. container plain yogurt. Pour into 4 dessert dishes. Chill in freezer for 25 minutes.

CARAMEL CUSTARD MOLD

1-1/2 cups sugar (divided use)
1 quart milk
6 eggs
1/8 tsp. salt
1 tsp. vanilla

Preheat oven to 325°.

To make caramelized sugar, place 1 cup sugar in heavy skillet; cook over low to medium heat, without stirring, until sugar had melted and begins to form light-brown syrup. Stir to blend. Use at once to coat 1-1/2 quart casserole, rotating dish until bottom and side are thoroughly coated.

In medium saucepan, over medium heat, heat milk just until bubbles form around edge of pan.

In large bowl, beat eggs slightly. Stir in 1/2 cup sugar, the salt and vanilla. Gradually add hot milk, stirring constantly. Pour into prepared dish.

Place in shallow pan; pour hot water to 1/2 inch depth around dish.

Bake 1 hour and 15 minutes, or until knife blade inserted deep near center of custard comes out clean. Cool. Refrigerate overnight.

To serve: Run small spatula around edge of dish to loosen. Invert onto shallow serving dish; shake gently to release. The caramel will serve as a sauce.

Yield: 8 servings

HOT FUDGE

2 oz. extra bittersweet chocolate (Tobler is the best)
2 Tbs. sweet butter
1/4 cup sugar
2 Tbs. light corn syrup
1/2 tsp. vanilla
Pinch of salt

In a small, heavy saucepan, combine the chocolate with 1/3 cup of water. Cook over low heat, stirring constantly, until the chocolate melts.

Add the butter, sugar, corn syrup, and salt. Simmer, stirring until the sugar melts, about 2 minutes.

Increase the heat to moderate and boil without stirring until the fudge thickens and reduces to a scant 2/3 cup, about 5 minutes.

Let cool slightly, then add the vanilla. The hot fudge should be very thick, but pourable.

The fudge can be made up to 5 days ahead. Pour into heat proof glass container and refrigerate, covered. Reheat in microwave oven or in a pan of hot water (double boiler) stirring, until pourable.

CHOCOLATE-COVERED ANYTHING

6 oz. semi-sweet chocolate chips

3 Tbs. vegetable shortening (Do not substitute butter or margarine)

Melt the chocolate and shortening in a small, heat proof bowl over simmering water or in the microwave. Remove from heat, but keep over hot water while you're working. Dip desired food into the chocolate, one at a time, lifting quickly from the mixture and tapping fork or tong lightly against the bowl to let excess chocolate drip off. Place on wire rack (to make cleanup easy, place rack on sheet of waxed paper). Store in a cool place or in the refrigerator.

Yield: Enough to dip 60 mini pretzels or 2 lbs. of fruit

RICE PUDDING

5 eggs
8 oz. sugar
Pinch of salt
Pinch of nutmeg
1 pint milk
1 oz. flour
1 oz. vanilla
1 cup cooked rice

Blend dry ingredients well. Add eggs. Then add all other ingredients. Add mixture to greased baking dish. Add cooked rice; pour over mixture. Cook at 225° for one hour.

CHOCOLATE MOUSSE

Melt in top of double boiler:
1 pkg. (6 oz.) chocolate chips.
Remove from heat
Beat in:
1 egg
2 egg yolks
1-1/2 tsp. rum
Fold in:
2 egg whites, stiffly beaten
1 cup whipped cream

Top with shaved bitter chocolate.

SMOOTH BAVARIAN CREAM

1 Tbs. gelatin
1/4 tsp. salt
2 Tbs. cold water
2 eggs, separated
1-1/3 cups milk
1 tsp. vanilla
1/2 cup sugar
1 cup whipping cream

Soften gelatin in cold water. Scald milk in top of double boiler. Add gelatin, sugar and salt. Stir until thoroughly dissolved.
Beat egg yolks slightly. Stir in a little of the hot milk mixture. Cook over hot, not boiling, water until slightly thickened, 4 to 5 minutes, stirring constantly. Remove from hot water and cool. When almost set, fold in stiffly beaten egg whites, vanilla and stiffly beaten whipped cream. Turn into molds and chill.

CHERRIES JUBILEE

1 can (16 or 17 oz.) dark, sweet cherries
1/4 cup sugar
1 cinnamon stick
2 strips lemon peel (2 inches)
1 Tbs. lemon juice
1 Tbs. cornstarch
1/4 cup brandy
Ice cream

Drain syrup from cherries into measuring cup; add enough water to equal 1 cup. In chafing dish or medium saucepan, combine sugar, syrup, lemon peel and cinnamon stick. Bring to a boil over medium-high heat. Reduce heat; cover and simmer 15 minutes. Discard lemon peel and cinnamon stick.
Mix cornstarch with lemon juice until smooth and add to syrup mixture, stirring constantly. Cook until mixture boils and thickens. Add drained cherries; heat thoroughly.
In small saucepan warm brandy (do not boil). Pour into hot cherries. Remove from heat. Holding pan away from your face, ignite with long match or taper. Serve over ice cream.

BRANDIED CHERRIES

1 (16 oz.) can pitted, Bing cherries, packed in heavy syrup
2 Tbs. sugar
3 Tbs. Kirsch or Cognac

Drain the cherries, reserving 1/2 cup of the syrup. In a medium saucepan, combine the reserved syrup with the sugar. Bring to a boil, stirring constantly to dissolve the sugar.
Add the cherries, cover and simmer for 1 minute. Remove from heat and with a slotted spoon, transfer the cherries to a heat proof one pint jar. Add the Kirsch or the Cognac.
Boil the syrup in the saucepan until it is reduced by half, to about 1/4 cup. Pour the reduced syrup over cherries. Cover tightly and swirl to mix thoroughly. Refrigerate for at least 12 hours and up to 3 months before using.
This makes a great topping for ice cream or roast duck. Serve over ice cream with a spoonful of hot fudge, whipped cream and chopped nuts.
Yield: 2 cups

PEARS HELENE

1-1/4 cups freshly squeezed orange juice
2 large pears, pared, cored and cut in half
1 (8 oz.) pkg. cream cheese, softened at room temperature
1/3 cup ground walnuts
2 Tbs. confectioner's sugar
1 pkg. (6 oz.) semisweet chocolate pieces
1 Tbs. grated orange rind

Dash of salt

In large saucepan bring orange juice to a boil. Add pears. Cover. Reduce heat; simmer 20 to 25 minutes or until pears are tender but hold their shape. Reserve 1/2 cup orange juice. Chill pears. In top of double boiler, melt chocolate over hot (not boiling) water. Add reserved 1/2 cup orange juice and salt; blend until smooth; set aside.

In small bowl beat cream cheese until smooth; blend in walnuts, confectioners' sugar and orange rind. Arrange pears in pool of chocolate sauce in dessert dishes. Pipe or spoon cream cheese mixture on top of pears.

Yield: 4 servings

PEAR PARFAIT

1 (16 oz.) can pear halves, drained
1 Tbs. lemon juice
1 cup sour cream
1 Tbs. sugar
1/8 tsp. ground nutmeg

In blender, puree pears with lemon juice until smooth. Combine sour cream, sugar and nutmeg. Place 2 tablespoons sour cream into each of 4 parfait glasses. Top with 2 tablespoons pear puree. Repeat layers. Serve well chilled.

DELICIOUS CARAMEL PEARS

1 (29 oz.) can pear halves, drained
2 Tbs. butter
3 Tbs. sugar
1/2 cup whipping cream
1/2 tsp. vanilla

Adjust broiler rack about 4 inches from heat source. Preheat broiler. Drain pears on paper towels. Grease an 8 inch square baking pan. Arrange pears in pan, cut side down and evenly sprinkle on sugar. Dot with butter. Broil 8 to 10 minutes, rotating pan to brown pears evenly. Remove from broiler. Reduce oven to 375°. Combine cream and vanilla; pour over pears. Return to oven and bake 10 minutes until sauce is golden and bubbly. Serve warm or at room temperature.

ICE CREAM CLAD IN CHOCOLATE

2 (8-1/2 oz.) pkgs. fine chocolate wafer crumbs
1 pint pistachio ice cream
2 pints vanilla ice cream, slightly softened
1 cup melted butter
2 pints chocolate ice cream
Coconut flakes

Combine crumbs and butter, reserve 2/3 cup of mixture. Firmly press remaining crumbs over bottom and sides of 9 inch spring form

pan. Freeze 15 minutes.

Stir vanilla ice cream to soften and spread over chilled crumbs. Sprinkle with half the reserved crumbs. Freeze firm.

Stir pistachio ice cream to soften; spread over vanilla layer; sprinkle with remaining crumbs and freeze firm. Spread softened chocolate ice cream over pistachio layer; freeze firm. Invert pan over chilled serving plate; release catch and remove sides and bottom of pan.
Garnish with wreath of coconut.

LEMON ICE

2-1/4 cups water
1-1/2 cups sugar
3/4 cups dry white wine
Grated rind from 6 lemons
1-1/4 to 1-1/2 cups fresh lemon juice

Heat water and sugar to boiling in saucepan. Boil for 3 minutes. Cool. Add all remaining ingredients. Freeze in a 9x13 inch pan.

Note:

Serve after pasta and before main course at dinner party. Serve in champagne glasses or sherbet dishes.

16 CAKES

& ICINGS

HINTS

Use all-purpose, unsifted flour unless otherwise specified.

Cake pans may be prepared for baking in one of three ways for easy removal of cake:

1. Grease bottom and sides of pan very well, using about 1/2 Tbs. shortening. Dust with flour until bottom and sides are well coated. Shake out excess flour.
2. Line with wax paper
3. Use a non-stick vegetable spray, or baking spray.

Never grease a tube pan when making sponge or chiffon cakes.

When making chocolate cake, use cocoa instead of flour for dusting pans.

Use standard measuring cups and spoons and measure accurately for best results.

Your cake is done when a knife or toothpick inserted in the center comes out dry. Also, the top of the cake will spring back when lightly touched.

Reduce oven temperature by 25 degrees when using glass baking pans.

When baking browns too quickly on top and is underdone in the center, place a pan of water above it. When the bottom browns too quickly, place a pan of water underneath.

Stale cake can be freshened by dipping in cold water for a second, then reheating slowly. Don't try any that have icings.

Juice (orange or apple) or milk to a cake mix instead of water will give that home-made taste.

If the top of your cake is humped or cracked, it may be from overmixing, using too much flour or too little liquid, or too high a temperature.

Soggy layer at the bottom of your cake? This can result from too much liquid, under-baking, undermixing, or underbeaten eggs.

When adding dry ingredients alternately with liquid, mix just until blended. Overbeating will reduce volume.

To make cupcakes and muffins uniform in size, use a 1/4 cup measuring cup to fill each compartment of muffin tin, making each compartment 2/3 full.

An easy way to measure shortening is to fill a 2 cup measuring cup with 1 cup cold water. Then add shortening (for 1/2 cup shortening, the water level will rise to 1-1/2 cups).

If a portion of egg yolk falls into the white, remove it with the egg shell; or a cloth dampened in cold water and touched to the yolk will also do the trick.

If baking powder has been on your shelf for a year or more, better replace it. It may have lost its strength.

To melt cooking chocolate or butter and not dirty a saucepan, place on a piece of tinfoil in the top of a double boiler.

Dip knife in cold water before cutting an iced cake.

Icing spreads easier when you dip knife in cold water.

To ice a cake easily, first place it on a lazy susan.

Chocolate curls: Melt a milk chocolate bar. Spread melted chocolate evenly over a strip of wax paper (cut to desired length and about 2 inches wide). Roll up jelly roll fashion and fasten securely with scotch tape. Freeze until firm. Remove paper and garnish cake.

BLUEBERRY COFFEE CAKE

3/4 cup sugar
1/4 cup shortening
1 egg
1/2 cup of milk
2 cups sifted flour
2 tsp. baking powder
1/2 tsp. salt
1 pint blueberries

Preheat oven to 350°. Mix sugar and shortening with an electric mixer; add the egg and milk.

Mix in the flour, baking powder and salt. Gently fold in the berries and pour into a greased 8 or 9 inch square baking dish.

Topping
1/2 tsp. cinnamon
1/4 cup dark brown sugar
1/4 cup sugar
1/4 cup margarine, softened
1/3 cup flour

Combine topping ingredients and spread over batter.

Bake for 45 to 50 minutes. Serve with butter.

FIVE-CUP HEAVENLY HASH

1 (11 oz.) can mandarin
    oranges, well-drained
1 (8 oz.) can pineapple
    chunks, well-drained
1 cup flaked coconut
1 cup miniature marshmal-
    lows
1 cup sour cream

Combine all ingredients and chill several hours or overnight.

FABULOUS CHEESECAKE

2 pkg. (8 oz. size) soft cream
    cheese
1 lb. creamed cottage cheese
1-1/2 cups sugar
4 eggs, slightly beaten
3 Tbs. cornstarch
3 Tbs. flour
1-1/2 Tbs. lemon juice
1 tsp. vanilla extract
1/2 cup butter or margarine,
    melted
1 pint dairy sour cream
Fresh strawberries, blueber-
    ries, or pineapple

Preheat oven to 325°. Grease a 9 inch spring form pan.

In a large bowl of electric mixer, at high speed, beat cream cheese with cottage cheese until creamy and well combined. Gradually beat in sugar; then beat in eggs until well combined.

At low speed, beat in cornstarch, four, lemon juice, and vanilla. Add melted butter and sour cream; beat just until smooth.

Pour into prepared pan; bake 1 hour and 10 minutes or until firm around the edges. Turn off oven. Let cake stand in oven 2 hours.

Remove cake from oven; let cool completely. Refrigerate until well chilled - several hours.

To serve: Run spatula around side of cheesecake, to loosen; remove side of spring form pan; leave bottom of pan in place. Serve with fresh strawberries, blueber- ries or pineapple.

MARBLE CHEESECAKE

1-1/2 cups graham cracker
    crumbs
1/4 cup sugar
6 Tbs. butter or margarine,
    melted
4 (8 oz.) pkgs. cream cheese,
    softened
2 tsp. vanilla
1-3/4 cups sugar
6 eggs
2 cups light cream
2 squares (2 oz.) unsweetened
    chocolate, melted

Combine cracker crumbs, 1/4 cup sugar, and butter or margarine. Press in bottom and 2 inches up sides of a 9 inch spring form pan; set aside. Beat cream cheese and vanilla till fluffy; gradually beat in sugar. Add eggs, one at a time, beating just till blended. Stir in cream. Combine about 3 cups of the batter with cooled chocolate. Pour plain cheese mixture into crust; gradually add chocolate mixture using zigzag motion. Bake in 450° oven for 15 minutes. Reduce heat to 300°, continue baking for 1 hour 10 minutes or till knife inserted halfway between center and edge comes out clean. Cool 1 hour; remove sides of pan. Chill cake.

Yield: 16 servings

HONEY CAKE

3 cups sifted flour
1 tsp. baking soda
2 tsp. baking powder
1 tsp. ginger
1 tsp. cinnamon
1/2 tsp. nutmeg
1/2 tsp. salt

Mix dry ingredients together; set aside.
3 eggs
1 cup sugar
1 cup honey
1 cup strong coffee
2 Tbs. oil
1/2 cut nuts

Beat liquids; then add dry ingredients. Bake in greased and floured 9 x 13 inch pan for 40 minutes at 350°.

SUNDAY CAKE

2/3 cup butter or margarine
2 eggs
1/2 tsp. baking powder
2/3 cup sugar
2/3 cup cake flour, sifted
1/4 tsp. vanilla
Few drops almond extract

Topping
2 Tbs. confectioner's sugar
1/2 tsp. grated orange rind
2 Tbs. orange juice

Grease and flour an 8 inch iron skillet. Cream the butter and sugar, then add the eggs, one at a time and beat thoroughly. Sift the dry ingredients and add slowly. Beat until smooth and add vanilla and almond extracts.

Pour into prepared skillet and bake about 30 minutes at 350°. Cook 10 minutes. Turn upside down on serving plate. Mix together topping ingredients and spoon over cake. Serve warm.

Note:
You may substitute a 9 inch cake pan for the skillet, but you won't get as crusty an outside.

PRALINE CAKE
Add 1 stick butter or margarine into 1 cup hot buttermilk. Add 2 cups brown sugar and stir until dissolved. Let cool.

Beat into mixture 2 eggs and 1 tsp. vanilla. Sift 2 cups flour, 1 Tbs. cocoa and 1 tsp. baking soda. Mix into batter. Turn into greased 13 x 9 pan. Bake 20 to 30 minutes at 350°.

Topping
Heat 1 stick margarine and 1 cup brown sugar until melted. Add 6 Tbs. cream or evaporated milk. Add 1 cup coconut, 1 cup broken pecans and 1 tsp. vanilla. Spread on cake while warm. Heat under broiler until coconut is toasted.

PINEAPPLE BARS (OR CAKE)

2 cups flour
2 cups sugar
2 beaten eggs
1 (20-1/2 oz.) can pineapple
  & juice
1 tsp. vanilla
2 tsp. baking soda
1/2 cups chopped nuts

Blend all of the above ingredients by hand (do not use mixer). Use pineapple and the juice (pineapple packed in its own juice is best). For bars put in greased 10 x 15 pan for 25 minutes at 350°. For cake, put in 10 x 10 pan for about 40 minutes at 350°. Frost with cream cheese icing.

Cream Cheese Icing
1 (8 oz.) pkg. cream cheese
1-3/4 cups powdered sugar
1/2 stick butter or margarine
1 tsp. vanilla
1/2 cup chopped nuts

Combine all - frost cake.

Notes:
In cake recipe, use only 1-1/2 cups sugar, 1 cup whole wheat flour and 1 cup regular white flour. Add a few fresh strawberries in the frosting for color and little flavor.

STRAWBERRY BLITZ TORTE

Cake Batter
1/2 cup butter
1/2 cup sugar
1/8 tsp. salt
4 egg yolks
1 tsp. vanilla
3 Tbs. milk
1 cup self rising flour

Cream butter, sugar and salt. Add egg yolks, milk, flour and vanilla. Pour batter in two round pans. (Use Pam or oil and flour pans.)

Meringue
4 egg whites
3/4 cup sugar
Slivered almonds
Cinnamon and sugar, mixed

Beat egg whites until stiff, gradually adding the sugar. Put stiff meringue on the unbaked cake batter. Sprinkle slivered almonds on the meringue. Top with a mixture of sugar and cinnamon.
Bake at 350° approximately 20 to 25 minutes until golden brown.

Filling
Large pkg. frozen strawberries
1 container whipped cream - whipped (1/2 pint size)

When cake is completely cooled, flip one layer so meringue side is down. Spread the thawed berries and juice on top of this layer. Add whipped cream and spread. Place second layer on top, meringue side up. Use all juice from berries.

APRICOT GOOEY CAKE

13 to 18 large dried apricot halves
1-2/3 cups sifted flour
1/2 tsp. baking powder
1/2 tsp. soda
1/2 tsp. salt
1 cup sugar
1/3 cup Crisco (or margarine or butter)
1 unbeaten egg
1/2 tsp. vanilla
1/4 tsp. lemon extract
3/4 cup water

Cook the dried apricot halves in water to cover until tender. Drain and mash thoroughly. Set aside.
Sift together the flour, baking powder, soda and salt. Set aside,
Cream the Crisco and the sugar. Add the egg and the extracts. Beat well.
Add to creamed mixture the dry ingredients alternately with the water, beginning and ending with the dry ingredients. Blend thoroughly after each addition.
Blend in 2 Tbs. of the mashed apricots thoroughly.
Turn into 9 x 9 x 2 or 11 x 7 x 2 pan, well greased and lightly floured in bottom only. Bake at 350° for 35 to 45 minutes. Cool, then add topping.

Apricot Coconut Topping
Combine 2 Tbs. butter, 1/4 cup firmly packed brown sugar and the remaining mashed apricots in a saucepan. Cook over medium heat for 3 minutes, stirring constantly. Remove from heat. Add 1/2 cup coconut, coarsely chopped. Spread over cake while topping is still warm.

Note:
This recipe was a Pillsbury bakeoff winner back in the 60's.

LILLY'S HUNGARIAN DOBOS TORTE

12 Tbs. sugar
12 eggs, separated
12 Tbs. all-purpose flour
1 tsp. vanilla

Beat egg yolks with electric mixer until thick and lemon colored. Gradually add sugar and continue beating for about 30 minutes. Beat egg whites until stiff and fold in alternately with the flour. Add vanilla. Bake layers in loose bottom pans or turn ordinary round cake pans upside down and spread batter about 1/4 inch thick. (For first few layers, duct with flour). Bake layers in moderate oven 350° for 10 to 12 minutes. Batter is sufficient for 8 or 9 layers. Remove pans by sliding spatula underneath. Cool on sheets of waxed paper.

Frost with following filling

Mix 1 lb. confectioner's sugar, 1/2 lb. butter, 3-1/2 Tbs. unsweetened cocoa, 1 tsp. vanilla and about 3 Tbs. hot black coffee. Beat until spreading consistency. Decorate top of cake with finely chopped walnuts.

COFFEE CAKE

1 pint milk
1-1/2 oz. yeast - dissolved in milk
Add:
6 cups flour
5 eggs
2 yolks
1 cup sugar
1-1/2 cups butter
1 Tsp. salt
Rind of 1 lemon
Pinch nutmeg

Mix all together until smooth. Pour into pans and let raise until twice natural size.
Bake at 325°.

AMARETTO CHEESECAKE

1-1/2 cups graham cracker crumbs
2 Tbs. sugar
1 tsp. ground cinnamon
1/4 cup plus 2 Tbs. butter or margarine, melted
3 (8 oz.) pkgs. cream cheese, softened
1 cup sugar
4 eggs
1/3 cup plus 1 Tbs. amaretto

1 (8 oz.) carton sour cream
1 Tbs. plus 1 tsp. sugar
1 Tbs. amaretto
1/4 cup toasted sliced almonds
1 (1.2 oz.) chocolate candy bar, grated

Combine graham cracker crumbs, 2 Tbs. sugar, cinnamon and butter; mix well. Firmly press mixture into bottom and 1/2 inch up sides of a 9 inch spring form pan.
Beat cream cheese with electric mixer until light and fluffy. Gradually add 1 cup sugar, mixing well. Add eggs, one at a time, beating well after each addition. Stir in 1/3 cup amaretto. Pour into prepared pan. Bake at 375° for 45 to 50 minutes or until set.
Combine sour cream, 1 Tbs. plus 1 tsp. sugar and 1 Tbs. amaretto; stir well and spoon over the cheesecake. Bake at 500° for 5 minutes. Let cool to room temperature; then refrigerate for 24 to 48 hours.
Cheesecake is best when thoroughly chilled and flavors have time to ripen. Garnish with toasted almonds and grated chocolate.
Yield: 12 servings

FRUIT CAKE

1-1/2 cups sugar
1 cup butter of shortening
5 eggs
1/4 pint milk
1 tsp. baking powder
3 cups flour, sifted

1/2 lemon
1/2 cup nuts
1/2 cup fruit
1/2 cup raisins
1/2 cup cherries

Mix flour and fruit together. Cream sugar with butter and flavoring. Add eggs slowly; cream until light. Add milk, then flour, fruit, nuts and baking powder. Mix till smooth. Bake at 300°.

MISSISSIPPI MUD CAKE

Cake
1 cup butter or margarine
2 cups granulated sugar
1/2 cup unsweetened cocoa powder
4 large eggs
2 tsp. vanilla extract
1-1/2 cups all-purpose flour
1/4 cup walnut pieces, chopped coarse
1/4 tsp. salt
1/2 cup miniature marshmallows

Frosting
1/2 cup butter or margarine
1/3 cup milk
1/4 cup unsweetened cocoa powder
1/2 tsp. vanilla extract
1 box (16 oz.) confectioner's sugar

To make cake, put butter in large mixing bowl. Microwave on high 1 to 1-1/2 minutes until melted. Stir in sugar and cocoa powder. Add eggs and vanilla; beat vigorously until well blended. Stir in flour, walnuts and salt. Let batter rest 10 minutes. Pour into an 11-3/4 x 7-1/2 inch baking dish. Place on a plastic trivet or inverted saucer in microwave oven. Microwave on medium 9 minutes, rotating dish 1/2 turn after 3 minutes. Shield the corners of the dish with small triangles of foil (don't let triangles touch each other or sides of oven). Microwave on high 3 to 5 minutes, rotating dish 1/2 turn once, until top is mostly dry with a few moist spots and pick inserted near center comes out clean.

Sprinkle marshmallows evenly over top of cake. Let stand about 5 minutes until marshmallows are slightly melted.

Meanwhile to make frosting, put butter in a large bowl. Microwave on high 30 to 60 seconds until melted. Stir in milk, cocoa powder and vanilla. Add sugar; beat vigorously until smooth. Spread evenly over marshmallows (cake will be warm). Let stand on flat heat proof surface 30 minutes until slightly warm, or cool completely and serve at room temperature.

Yield: 16 servings

HOT FUDGE SAUCE

2 cups sugar
2/3 cup unsweetened cocoa
6 Tbs. all-purpose flour
1 tsp. salt
2 cups homogenized milk
2 Tbs. butter or margarine
2 tsp. vanilla

Mix dry ingredients in saucepan. Add milk. Cook over medium heat, stirring constantly, until thick. Remove from heat and add butter and vanilla. Stir until blended. Pour into jar and refrigerate. Serve hot or cold. Keeps well.

AMARETTO-CHOCOLATE SAUCE

1 cup whipping cream
1/3 cup sugar
2 (4 oz.) bittersweet chocolate bars, chopped
2 Tbs. butter or margarine
3 to 4 Tbs. amaretto
Garnish: fresh strawberries

Combine first 4 ingredients in a small saucepan. Cook over low heat, stirring constantly, until thickened and smooth. Remove from heat, and stir in liqueur. Serve warm or at room temperature.

CHOCOLATE-SOUR CREAM POUND CAKE

1 cup butter or margarine, softened
2 cups sugar
1 cup firmly packed brown sugar
6 large eggs
2-1/2 cups all-purpose flour
1/4 tsp. baking soda
1/2 cup cocoa
1 (8 oz.) carton sour cream
2 tsp. vanilla extract
Powdered sugar (optional)

Beat butter at medium speed with an electric mixer about 2 minutes or until soft and creamy. Gradually add sugars, beating at medium speed 5 to 7 minutes. Add eggs, one at a time, beating just until yellow disappears.

Combine flour, baking soda, and cocoa; add to creamed mixture alternately with sour cream, beginning and ending with flour mixture. Mix at lowest speed just until blended after each addition. Stir in vanilla.

Spoon batter into a greased and floured 10 inch tube pan. Bake at 325° for 1 hour and 20 minutes or until a wooden pick inserted in center comes out clean. Cool in pan on a wire rack for 10 to 15 minutes. Remove from pan, and cool completely on a wire rack. Sprinkle with powdered sugar, if desired.

Yield: one 10 inch cake

CHOCOLATE SHEET CAKE

1/3 cup all-purpose flour
1/4 cup unsweetened cocoa powder
6 egg yolks
2 Tbs. sugar
5 egg whites
1/4 cup sugar

Grease and line a 15 x 10 x 1 inch baking pan with waxed

paper; grease and flour paper. Set pan aside.

In a small mixing bowl stir together flour and cocoa powder; set aside.

In a medium mixing bowl combine egg yolks and the 2 Tbs. sugar; beat with an electric mixer on high speed about 5 minutes or till thick and light colored. Wash beaters.

In a large mixing bowl, beat egg whites on medium speed till soft peaks form (tips curl). Gradually add the 1/4 cup sugar, beating on high speed till stiff peaks form (tips stand straight).

Using a spatula, fold beaten whites into yolk mixture. Sprinkle flour mixture over egg mixture; gently fold till combined. Pour batter into prepared pan; spread evenly.

Bake in a 350° oven for 10 to 12 minutes or till cake springs back when touched and a wooden toothpick inserted near center comes out clean.

Cook cake in pan on wire racks for 5 minutes; use a knife to loosen edges and remove from pan. Cook completely on wire racks.

Yield: One sheet cake

DUTCH APPLE CAKE

1/3 cup milk
1/4 cup sugar
1/2 tsp. salt
4 Tbs. butter
1/4 cup warm water
1 pkg. yeast
1 egg, beaten

1-1/3 cups sifted flour
1-1/2 cups apple slices
4 Tbs. brown sugar
1/4 tsp. cinnamon
1/4 tsp. nutmeg

Scald milk, stir in sugar, salt and two Tbs. of the butter. Cool to lukewarm. Dissolve yeast in water. Stir in lukewarm milk mixture. Add egg and flour. Beat until smooth.

Spread dough evenly in greased 9 x 9 x 2 inch pan. Arrange apple slices on top. Sprinkle with mixture of brown sugar, cinnamon and nutmeg. Dot with remaining butter.

Cover, let rise in warm place until double, about 40 minutes, or more. Bake in preheated 400° oven 25 minutes.

BANANA CHOCOLATE CHIP CAKE

1-1/4 cups sugar
1/2 cup butter
2 eggs
1 tsp. soda
1 tsp. vanilla
3/4 cup chocolate chips
4 Tbs. sour cream
1 cup bananas (2 medium)
1-1/2 cups flour
1/4 tsp. salt

Cream butter and sugar. Add eggs and soda dissolved in sour cream. Beat well. Add banana, flour, salt and vanilla. Mix well.

Bake in 9 x 9 square pan

that has been greased and floured. Add 3/4 cup chocolate chips. Sprinkle top with powdered sugar.

Bake at 350° for 40 to 45 minutes.

CHOCOLATE CHIP CINNAMON SQUARES

2 cups flour
1 tsp. baking powder
1 cup sugar
3 tsp. cinnamon
1/2 cup butter or margarine
1/2 cup shortening
1 egg plus 1 yolk
1 beaten egg white

Topping
1 pkg. chocolate chips
1 cup chopped nuts
1/3 cup sugar
1 tsp. cinnamon

Preheat oven to 350°. Sift together all dry ingredients. Add butter, shortening, 1 egg and 1 egg yolk and beat on low until well-blended.

Turn into greased jelly-roll pan (15 x 10 x 3/4). Spread evenly. Brush on 1 beaten egg white. Sprinkle on topping.

Bake for 22 minutes. Cool on rack. Cut into squares while warm. Leave in pan until completely cooled.

SWEET TREATS

1/2 cup butter
1-1/2 cups brown sugar
    (packed)
1 cup flour
2 eggs
2 Tbs. vanilla
3/4 cup chopped pecans

Cream butter and 1/2 cup sugar. Add flour and mix thoroughly. Press into greased 8 x 8 inch pan. Bake 20 minutes at 350°. Cool.

Beat eggs and remaining sugar. Add vanilla and nuts. Spread on crust. Bake 20 minutes at 350°. After removing from oven, cut around edge. Cool 10 minutes. Cut into squares. Put confectioner's sugar on top when cool.

LITTLE BASKETS

1 (3 oz.) pkg. cream cheese
1/4 cup butter
1 cup sifted flour

Beat cream cheese in small bowl until creamy. Add butter. Blend well. Mix in flour. Work mixture with hands into little balls. Press dough into 1-3/4 inch muffin tins. Bake at 400° for 20 minutes.
    Yield: 30 baskets

Cheese Filling
6 oz. cream cheese
1/2 cup sugar
1 egg
1 Tbs. lemon rind

1 Tbs. lemon juice

Chocolate-Nut Filling
2 egg whites beaten stiff. Add 1/3 cup sugar gradually. Fold in 1/4 cup chopped nuts and 1/4 cup chocolate chips.

DREAM BARS

First Layer
1/2 cup (1 stick) butter or
    margarine
1/2 cup brown sugar, packed
1-1/2 cups all-purpose flour

Cream together the butter and brown sugar until light, then cut in the flour until crumbly. Pat into a lightly greased 9 x 13 inch pan and bake 10 minutes at 350°.

Second Layer
2 eggs
1 cup brown sugar, packed
1/2 tsp. salt
1 tsp. vanilla
2 Tbs. all-purpose flour
1/2 tsp. baking powder
1/2 to 1-1/2 cups flaked
    coconut (to taste)
1 cup chopped pecans

Beat together the eggs, sugar, salt and vanilla until foamy. Mix the flour and baking powder together. Toss with the coconut and pecans. Stir the 2 mixtures together, then pour over the first layer.

Return to oven and bake 20 to 25 additional minutes, or until golden brown and firm to touch.

Let cool slightly before cutting into bars. Cool completely before removing from pan.
    Yield: 24 bars

BROWNIES

3-1/4 cups sugar
3/4 cup shortening
1 cup butter
1/3 cup corn syrup
2-1/2 oz. unsweetened baking chocolate, melted
1-3/4 cups eggs (about 9
    large)
1 tsp. baking powder
1/4 tsp. baking soda
1/2 tsp. salt
1/2 cup cocoa powder
1-1/4 cups walnuts
1-3/4 to 2 cups cake flour

Cream sugar, shortening and butter until light and fluffy. Add corn syrup. Mix and scrape down the sides of the bowl. Add melted chocolate and mix well. Scrape down the sides of the bowl again. Gradually add eggs, mixing well. Stir the remaining ingredients together and stir into the batter, mixing only until ingredients are incorporated.

Pour batter into a greased 9 x 13 inch pan and bake 20 to 25 minutes at 350°.
    Yield: 18 brownies

TURTLE BROWNIES

1 (14 oz.) pkg. caramels
2/3 cup evaporated milk
3/4 cup softened margarine
1 cup nuts (walnuts and/or
  pecans)
1 box (18-1/2 oz.) German
  chocolate cake mix
12 oz. semisweet chocolate
  pieces

Combine caramels and 1/3 cup evaporated milk on top of double boiler. Stir mixture until melted.

Combine cake mix, remaining milk and softened margarine. Blend until mixture holds together. Stir in nuts. Press one-half of the cake mixture in a greased 13 x 9 inch pan and bake for 6 minutes at 350°. Remove from oven and sprinkle chocolate pieces on top. Pour melted caramel evenly over top. Crumble remaining mix over caramel and bake at 350° for 15 to 20 minutes. Cool slightly and cut into bars. Serve.

BONNA'S CHEESE CAKE

3 (8 oz. each) pkgs. cream
  cheese
1 cup sugar
3 eggs
3/4 tsp. rum

Let cheese soften and whip well with rum. Gradually add sugar and eggs, one at a time. Beat together for 30 minutes. Pour into graham cracker crust and bake for 30 minutes at 375°.

While this is baking, blend the following as topping:
1 pint sour cream
1 tsp. vanilla
3 Tbs. sugar

When pie has baked 30 minutes, spread this topping all over fast. Put back in oven for 5 to 15 minutes. Remove and cool.

FANNY'S CHEESE CAKE

1/2 lb. riced cream cheese
1/2 pint sour cream
1 lb. large curb cottage cheese
3 eggs
1 cup sugar
3 Tbs. flour
1/8 lb. butter

Mix together; mixture will be thin. Let set for 1/2 hour. Bake in graham cracker crust for 1 hour at 350°.

IMPOSSIBLE CHEESECAKE

3/4 cup sugar
2 tsp. vanilla
1/2 cup Bisquick baking mix
1/2 tsp. grated lemon peel
2 eggs
2 pkgs. (8 oz. each) cream
  cheese, cut into 1 inch cubes
  and softened
Cheesecake topping

Heat oven to 350°. Grease a 9 inch pie plate. Place all ingredients except topping in blender container. Blend on High speed, stopping blender occasionally to stir, until smooth, about 3 minutes. (Or beat in large bowl on high speed for 2 minutes, scraping bowl constantly.) Pour into pie plate. Bake just until puffed and center is dry, about 30 minutes. (Do not overbake.) Spread cheesecake topping carefully over top; cool. Refrigerate until chilled, at least 3 hours.

Topping
Mix 1 cup sour cream, 2 Tbs. sugar and 2 tsp. vanilla

HOLIDAY CHOCOLATE LOG

Log
6 egg whites (see Note)
3/4 cup sugar
1/3 cup unsweetened cocoa
6 egg yolks
1-1/2 tsp. vanilla
Confectioner's sugar

Filling
1-1/2 cups heavy cream,
  chilled
1/2 cup confectioner's sugar
1/4 cup unsweetened cocoa
2 tsp. instant coffee
1 tsp. vanilla
Candied cherries, angelica

Note:
Let egg whites warm to room temperature — about 1 hour. You may make the log

a week ahead, then freeze it, wrapped in foil. Let stand at room temperature to thaw 1 hour before serving.

Grease bottom of a 15-1/2 x 10-1/2 x 1 inch jelly roll pan. Line with waxed paper. Grease lightly. Preheat the oven to 375°. In a large electric mixing bowl, at high speed, beat egg whites just until soft peaks form when the beater is slowly raised.

Add 1/4 cup sugar, 2 Tbs. at a time, beating until stiff peaks form when beater is slowly raised. With same beaters, beat yolks at high speed, adding remaining 1/2 cup sugar, 2 Tbs. at a time. Beat until mixture is very thick — about 4 minutes.

At low speed, beat in cocoa, vanilla and salt just until smooth. With wire whisk, or rubber scraper, using an under and over motion, gently fold the cocoa mixture into the beaten egg whites, just until they are blended (no egg white should show).

Spread evenly in pan. Bake 15 minutes. Just until surface springs back when gently pressed with fingertip. Sift confectioner's sugar in a 15 x 10 inch rectangle on clean linen towel. Turn cake out on sugar; lift off pan; peel paper off cake.

Roll up jelly-roll fashion, starting with the short end, towel and all. Cool completely on rack seam side down at least 1/2 hour. To make the filling; combine ingredients in medium bowl. Beat with electric mixer until

thick, and then refrigerate.

Unroll cake; spread with filling to 1 inch from edge. Reroll. Place seam side down on plate; cover loosely with foil. Refrigerate 1 hour before serving. To serve: sprinkle with confectioner's sugar; decorate with angelica cherries.

Yield: 10 servings

CHOCOLATE FRENCH COFFEE CAKE

1 (6 oz.) can evaporated milk, divided
3/4 cup sugar
4-1/2 cups sifted flour, divided
1/2 tsp. salt
1 (6 oz.) pkg. chocolate chips
4 egg yolks
1/2 tsp. cinnamon
2 pkgs. yeast
1/2 cup soft butter
1/2 cup warm water

Reserve 1/4 cup evaporated milk. Add water to remaining milk to make 1/2 cup. Combine with sugar, salt and egg yolks in large bowl. Beat well. Add butter and 2 cups flour. Beat until smooth.

Sprinkle yeast into warm water; stir until dissolved. Add yeast and 1 more cup flour to first mixture; beat at medium speed for 3 minutes.

Blend in remaining 1-1/2 cups flour. Cover. Let rise in warm place until double in bulk; about 1-1/2 hours.

Heat reserved 1/4 cup

evaporated milk in small saucepan just to boiling; remove from heat. Add chocolate chips and cinnamon. Stir until mixture is smooth.

Cool to room temperature. Punch down dough, turn out on well-floured surface; let rest a few minutes. Knead lightly a few times. Roll into 10 x 15 inch rectangle. Spread with chocolate mixture; roll up from long side like a jelly roll. Place roll seam down in greased 10 inch tube pan. Press ends together to seal. Sprinkle with Crumb Topping. Cover; let rise in warm place until double in bulk, about 1 hour.

Bake at 350° for 45 minutes. Carefully remove from pan.

Crumb Topping
1/2 cup flour
1/2 cup walnuts
1/3 cup sugar
1/4 cup soft butter
1/2 cup chocolate chips
1-1/2 tsp. cinnamon

Mix all ingredients with fork until well blended and crumbly.

WHITE CAKE

1/2 lb. butter
1-1/3 cup sugar
2-1/4 cup sifted cake flour
3 tsp. baking powder
1/4 tsp. salt
1 cup milk
1 tsp. vanilla
3 egg whites

Cream butter. Add sugar, flour, baking powder and salt alternately with milk and vanilla. Fold in stiffly beaten egg whites. Bake in 2 greased 8 inch pans for 25 to 30 minutes at 350°.

CHOCOLATE ICING I (COOKED)

1 square unsweetened chocolate
1 lump butter
1 Tbs. cocoa (heaping)
Confectioner's sugar

Melt chocolate and butter in double boiler; remove from heat. Add cocoa and enough confectioner's sugar and boiling water to make proper mixture.

CHOCOLATE ICING II (NO COOKING)

2 Tbs. cocoa (heaping)
1 egg-size lump butter
3/4 box confectioner's sugar
Boiling water

Mix thoroughly to make proper mixture.

CHOCOLATE ICING III (CORNSTARCH)

3 squares unsweetened chocolate
1 cup sugar
3 Tbs. cornstarch
1/2 cup milk
2 Tbs. butter

1 tsp. vanilla
2 Tbs. cold water

Melt chocolate in saucepan; add sugar and milk, stirring constantly. Mix cornstarch with cold water; add slowly to chocolate mixture; cook until thick. Remove from heat; mix in butter and vanilla.

CHOCOLATE FROSTING (SEVEN STARS)

1 (8 oz.) pkg. cream cheese
1 Tbs. milk
3 squares melted unsweetened chocolate, slightly cooled
1 tsp. vanilla
Dash of salt
1 lb. confectioner's sugar, sifted

Blend all ingredients well.

CHOCOLATE PECAN TORTE WITH STRAWBERRY CREAM

3/4 cup unsalted butter, softened
8 eggs
2 cups sugar
2 tsp. vanilla
1/4 tsp. salt
3-1/2 cups pecan halves, finely ground
12 oz. bittersweet or semisweet chocolate, melted
Strawberry Buttercream
Chocolate Glaze

7 or 8 strawberries for garnish

Preheat oven to 375°. Butter four 9 inch round cake pans. Line bottom with parchment paper; butter parchment.

Cream 3/4 cup butter until light; add sugar and beat until light and fluffy. Beat in eggs one at a time. Add vanilla and salt; beat. Stir in chocolate and pecans, mix well.

Divide batter into pans and bake about 22 minutes (top may crack). Cool in pans 5 minutes. Run knife around edge of cakes and invert onto racks. Discard parchment. Cool layers completely.

Place 1 layer bottom side up on platter. Slide strips of wax paper under edge of cake to keep platter clean during glazing. Spread 2/3 cup Strawberry Buttercream over layer. Repeat with remaining layers and Strawberry Buttercream, ending with cake layer bottom side up. Pat layers to even. Cover and refrigerate for at least 6 hours.

Before glazing, trim sides with serrated knife to even. Pour Chocolate Glaze over cake and smooth over sides and top. Remove wax paper. Arrange strawberries around top edge. Refrigerate, but let stand at room temperature 1 hour before serving.

Strawberry Buttercream

Cream 1-1/4 cups unsalted butter at room temperature and 2 cups sifted confectioner's sugar until light and fluffy. Mix in 4 egg yolks, 1/2 cup pureed fresh strawberries and 3 Tbs. strawberry preserves. Cover tightly and refrigerate until set. Before assembling, soften buttercream at room temperature until spreadable.

Chocolate Glaze

Heat 3 oz. semisweet chocolate, 1/2 cup water, 6 Tbs. unsalted butter and 3 Tbs. safflower oil in top of double boiler over gently simmering water until chocolate melts. Remove from heat. Add 3/4 cups unsweetened cocoa powder and 1/2 cup plus 2 Tbs. sugar until sugar dissolves and glaze is smooth. Let cool until thickened, but still pourable.

REAL BUTTER FROSTING

1/2 cup butter
1 egg
1 lb. confectioner's sugar
1 tsp. vanilla
1/2 tsp. salt
1 Tbs. milk

Cream butter. Add 1/3 sugar to butter, cream. Add salt, milk and vanilla. Blend unbeaten egg until smooth. Add rest of sugar gradually and beat until smooth.

BUTTER FROSTING

2 cups sifted confectioner's sugar
1/2 stick butter
2 to 3 Tbs. milk or cream
Dash of salt
1/2 tsp. vanilla

Cream butter and add 1 cup sugar. Add vanilla, salt and milk. Mix well. Blend in remaining sugar. Tint with color if desired.

BUTTER ORNAMENTAL FROSTING

3 cups sifted confectioner's sugar
1/2 stick butter
1-1/2 tsp. vanilla
2 Tbs. cream

Melt butter in upper part of double boiler over boiling water. Stir in sugar, cream and vanilla. Remove from heat and beat until have texture of spreading consistency. If necessary, stiffen with additional sugar. For decorating, frosting must be very stiff.

COOKIE DECORATING ICING

2 cups powdered sugar
1 Tbs. cream
1/4 cup butter
1 tsp. vanilla

Cream butter until soft. Add sugar, vanilla and cream. Beat until light and fluffy. Pack into cookie gun and decorate.

DECORATOR FROSTING

1-3/4 cup sifted powdered sugar
1 egg white
Food color

Beat egg slightly with fork. Gradually beat in sugar. Use cake decorator to frost.

CHOCOLATE RIBBON CAKE

1 prepared cake

Frosting
6 Tbs. unsalted butter
1 cup powdered sugar
1/2 cup unsweetened chocolate, melted
2 eggs
2 Tbs. hot tap water
1 tsp. vanilla

Melt chocolate over double boiler. Mix butter, sugar and tap water and add melted chocolate. Beat in eggs one at a time, add vanilla until it forms a consistency, then frost cake.

Chocolate Glaze
1 cup melted semi-sweet chocolate
1/4 cup tap water

Combine melted chocolate with water and mix until smooth. Glaze frosted cake by pouring glaze over cake then decorate with any goodies you might enjoy using. Lady Fingers around the sides make a very festive look. Fresh flowers, fresh fruit, chocolate shavings, nuts candies, cookies and ribbons are optional decorations.

TURTLE CAKE

1 box German Chocolate
   Cake mix
1 cup milk
1 pkg. (14 oz.) caramel candy
1 cup chocolate chips
1 cup nuts, chopped

Mix cake according to directions. Pour 1/2 of the mixture in a greased and floured 13 x 9 inch pan. Bake 10 minutes at 350°. Melt caramels with milk over low heat to make a sauce. Remove cake from the oven after 10 minutes and pour sauce over the cake. Sprinkle with chocolate chips and nuts. Pour remaining batter over cake and sauce. Bake an additional 17 to 20 minutes longer or until done.

CREAM CHEESE SWIRL COFFEE CAKE

2 (3 oz.) pkgs. cream cheese,
   softened
2 Tbs. confectioner's sugar
2 cups unsifted flour

2 Tbs. lemon juice
1 tsp. baking powder
1 tsp. baking soda
1 cup sugar
1/2 cup butter, softened
3 eggs
1 tsp. vanilla
1/4 tsp. salt
1 (8 oz.) container sour cream
Cinnamon-Nut Topping

Preheat oven to 350°. In small bowl, beat cheese, confectioner's sugar and lemon juice until smooth. Set aside. Stir together flour, baking powder, baking soda and salt, set aside. In large mixing bowl, beat granulated sugar and butter until fluffy. Add eggs and vanilla; mix well. Add dry ingredients alternately with sour cream; mix well. Pour half of batter into greased and floured 10 inch tube pan. Spoon cheese mixture on top of batter to within 1/2 inch of pan edge. Sprinkle with Cinnamon-Nut topping. Bake 40 to 45 minutes. Cook 10 minutes; remove from pan.

Cinnamon-Nut Topping
Combine:
1/4 cup finely chopped nuts
2 Tbs. sugar
1/2 tsp. ground cinnamon

SOUR CREAM COFFEE CAKE

1 cup butter
1 cup sugar
1 tsp. vanilla
3 tsp. baking powder

3 cups flour
3 eggs
1 cup (8 oz.) sour cream
1 tsp. baking soda

Topping
1 cup chopped nuts
1/4 cup sugar
1 square shaved chocolate or
1/2 cup mini chocolate chips

Cream butter, sugar and eggs. While beating, add dry ingredients alternately with sour cream. Add vanilla. Grease a spring form pan. Divide the batter into 3 parts. Put the first part in pan and sprinkle with 1/3 of the topping mixture. Add additional batter, 1/3 topping and repeat again. Bake in 350° for 1 hour.

CHOCOLATE COFFEECAKE

Filling
3/4 cup firmly packed light
   brown sugar
1/2 cup finely chopped dried
   apricots
1/2 cup coarsely chopped
   walnuts
2 oz. (about 1/3 cup) semi-
   sweet chocolate chips
2 Tbs. unsweetened cocoa
   powder
1 Tbs. instant coffee powder
2 tsp. cinnamon

In a medium bowl, combine all the ingredients and set aside.

Cake Batter

2-3/4 cups all-purpose flour
1-1/2 tsp. baking powder
1-1/2 tsp. baking soda
3/4 tsp. salt
1-1/2 cups granulated sugar
1 tsp. vanilla
3 large eggs
2 cups plain yogurt
12 Tbs. (1-1/2 sticks) unsalted butter at room
   temperature

Preheat oven to 350°. Position rack in center of oven. Generously butter the inside of a 10 inch bundt pan and lightly dust with flour.

In a medium bowl, stir together the flour, baking soda, baking powder, and salt. Sift together onto a large sheet of waxed paper.

In a large bowl, cream the butter, sugar and vanilla at medium speed for 3 minutes, until very light and fluffy. One at a time, add the eggs, beating well after each addition.

At low speed, one third at a time, add the sifted flour mixture alternately with the yogurt, beating after each addition. Beat just until the mixture is smooth.

Spread one-third of the batter over the bottom of the bundt pan. Sprinkle half of the filling evenly over the batter. Top with another one-third of the batter and sprinkle with the remaining filling. Top with the remaining batter and spread evenly.

Bake for 55 to 60 minutes. Cool on wire rack for 10 minutes. Invert cake onto the rack and cool at least 10 minutes more before slicing. Sift confectioner's sugar over top of cake.

CELESTIAL LEMON ROLL

Lemon Filling

3 Tbs. cornstarch
1/3 cup granulated sugar
1 tsp. grated lemon zest
1/3 cup fresh lemon juice
1 jumbo egg yolk
1 Tbs. unsalted butter

In a small heavy saucepan, combine the cornstarch and granulated sugar. Whisk in the lemon zest, lemon juice and 3/4 cup of water. Cook, stirring, over moderate heat until the mixture boils and is thick and smooth, about 3 minutes. Blend a little of the hot mixture into the egg yolk and scrape the warmed yolk back into the pan. Cook over low heat, stirring constantly, for 1 minute. Remove from heat and stir in the butter. Let cool to room temperature, stirring often to prevent a skin from forming. Cover and refrigerate. (The filling can be made a day ahead.) Return to room temperature and stir to restore to a spreading consistency before proceeding.

Angel Food Cake Roll

4 jumbo egg whites
1/8 tsp. salt
1/8 tsp. cream of tartar
1/2 cup sifted superfine
   sugar
1/2 cup sifted cake flour
1/2 tsp. vanilla extract
2 tsp. fresh lemon juice
1/4 tsp. almond extract
3 Tbs. confectioner's sugar

Preheat oven to 300°. Spray a 15-1/2 x 10-1/2 x 1 inch jelly roll pan lightly with non-stick spray and line the bottom and sides with parchment or waxed paper. Grease the paper lightly with a non-stick spray.

In a large bowl, beat the egg whites with the salt and cream of tartar until the egg whites bubbles are tiny and of even size and will mound when turned with a spatula, about 1 minute.

With a rubber spatula, gently fold in the superfine sugar, 2 Tbs. at a time. Sift the flour, about 2 Tbs. at a time, over the egg whites and fold in gently. When all of the flour is incorporated, fold in the lemon juice, vanilla and almond extract.

FRENCH STYLE YEAST DOUGH COFFEE CAKE

1 pkg. yeast
1/2 tsp. sugar
2 tsp. lukewarm water
1 tsp. flour

Mix together. Let stand in warm place until mixture rises to top of cup.

2 Tbs. sugar
3 cups flour
1/2 lb. plus 2 Tbs. butter
1/2 tsp. salt
1/4 cup lukewarm water
3 egg yolks

Blend together well. Add yeast mixture. Refrigerate overnight. Roll dough as for pie. Spread filling over dough and roll as a jelly roll. Place in greased 9 inch ring mold. Let rise for 3 hours. Bake 45 minutes at 350°. Frost if desired.

Filling
3 egg whites, beaten
3/4 cup sugar
1 cup crushed nuts
1/2 tsp. cinnamon
1 bar grated bittersweet chocolate

Add sugar gradually to egg whites. Add remainder of ingredients.

ICE BOX YEAST DOUGH

1/2 lb. butter
1 tsp. salt
1/2 cup sugar
1 cup milk, scalded
4 cups flour
1 pkg. yeast
2 eggs, beaten

Dissolve yeast with 1 tsp. sugar and 1 Tbs. warm water. Let stand.
Combine butter, salt and sugar. Pour warm milk over this. Add eggs and yeast

mixture. Add flour. Mix well and refrigerate overnight.

Swedish Ring
Roll out part of dough into 12 to 14 inch pie shape. Spread with liquid butter or sour cream, brown sugar and nuts. Roll like strudel and make round ring. Place on cookie sheet. Cut with shears 2 inch pieces — 1 inch from ring. Let rise until double in bulk. Bake 30 to 40 minutes at 350°.

PHILADELPHIA STICKY BUNS

1/4 cup sugar
1/2 tsp. salt
1 envelope rapid-rise dry yeast
2-1/4 to 2-1/2 cups all-purpose flour
1/4 cup milk
7 Tbs. unsalted butter, softened
1 egg, lightly beaten, room temperature
1/2 cup dark corn syrup
1/3 cup dark brown sugar (packed)
1 tsp. cinnamon
1/3 cups raisins
1/3 cup chopped nuts

In a large bowl, combine the sugar, salt, yeast and 1-1/4 cups of the flour. Mix well and set aside.
In a small heavy saucepan, combine the milk, 4 Tbs. of the butter and 1/4 cup of the water. Heat until the liquid

registers 125 to 130 degrees on an instant reading thermometer (approximately 5 minutes). Stir into the dry ingredients. Add the beaten egg and stir in enough additional flour to form a soft dough. Turn the dough out onto a lightly floured surface and knead until it becomes smooth and elastic, 8 to 10 minutes.

Place the dough in a greased bowl and cover with a damp towel. Set in a warm place and let rise until doubled, about 40 minutes.

Grease a 9 inch square baking pan. Pour the corn syrup into the pan and tip to coat evenly. Punch the dough down and turn out onto a lightly floured surface. Form the dough into a 9 inch square. Spread the remaining 3 tablespoons of butter over the dough. Sprinkle evenly with the brown sugar, cinnamon, raisins and nuts. Roll jelly-roll style and cut into 9 slices, each 1 inch thick.

Place the buns, flat-side down, in a single layer in rows of 3, in the prepared pan. Cover and set in warm place; let rise until doubled, 30 to 45 minutes.

Preheat the oven to 350°. Bake the buns for 25 to 30 minutes or until lightly browned. Remove from the oven and invert immediately onto a rack; leave the pan in place for 5 to 10 minutes to drain the syrup over the buns. Serve warm or at room temperature.

17 COOKIES

& BARS

HINTS

Store crisp cookies in a loosely covered container, and soft cookies in an airtight one.

Wrapping in tinfoil will keep biscuits and crackers crisp.

Cookies softened during storage? To restore crispness, place in a 300 degree oven for 5 minutes.

If you are making rolled cookies, make sure board and rolling pin are well floured. Cut as many as possible from each rolling to save time.

For best results, cookie sheets should be bright and shiny.

To prevent overbrowning of bottoms of cookies, use 2 pans the same size placed one on top of the other.

If you need extra cookie sheets, turn baking pans with sides upside down and bake cookies on the bottoms.

Cookies bake quickly - use a timer as a reminder.

Use a variety of cookie cutters for eye appeal.

Spatulas are ideal for lifting unbaked cookies onto pans and for removing hot ones from pans onto racks to cool.

If you are mailing cookies, use a heavy box and line it with wax paper. Use lots of filler (crushed paper, or unbuttered popcorn). Place cookies back to back in pairs, and wrap each pair. Place a layer of filler on the bottom of the box; pack cookies in layers with filler in between. Pad top with more filler, packing tightly to prevent contents from moving around.

HINTS

To mail fudge, grease a tin box and line with wax paper. Pour in hot fudge and mark in squares. Cool, then cover.

To melt chocolate, place on a piece of wax paper in the top of a double boiler.

To color coconut, sprinkle it on wax paper. Then add a little food coloring and rub evenly throughout. Dry and store in jars.

To color sugar, place some granulated sugar on wax paper. Sprinkle a few drops of food coloring over it and rub with a wooden spoon until color is even. Dry in a moderate oven, occasionally rubbing grains through the fingers to separate.

If brown sugar has hardened, rub the solid chunk back and forth against a grater over a bowl.

Unbaked dough for cookies may be frozen up to 9 months. Baked cookies may be frozen for 6 months.

To toast coconut, heat it in a shallow pan at 350°, stirring often, until golden.

To blanche almonds, remove shells. Pour boiling water over nuts and let stand 3 to 5 minutes, until skins are loosened. Drain off hot water and add some cold. Slip off skins and place nuts on paper toweling to dry.

To sliver blanched almonds, cut with a very sharp knife while moist and warm.

Place nuts in a plastic bag before crushing with a rolling pin to avoid messy cleanups.

To make sure nuts taste fresh, heat thoroughly at 350°.

Store shelled nuts (and coconut) tightly covered in the refrigerator or freezer. This will prevent the nuts from becoming rancid.

When making candies and icings, a candy thermometer is a great help.

HOW TO TURN CAKE MIX INTO COOKIES

Add 1 or 2 eggs, 2 Tbs. butter, and 2 Tbs. water to any cake mix. For really soft cookies, use 1/4 cup water.

Form dough into a roll. Chill in refrigerator. Slice or drop from a spoon for drop cookies; roll into balls and flatten if you want to decorate cookies.

Bake at 375° for approximately 8 minutes.

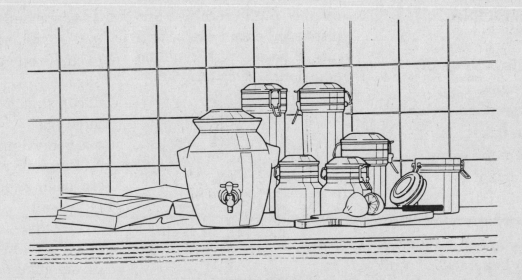

SOUR CREAM DROP COOKIES

1/4 sup soft butter
1/2 tsp. salt
1 cup sugar
1/2 tsp. baking soda
1 egg
1 cup sour cream
2 cups sifted flour
Cinnamon-sugar mixture

Cream butter and sugar until light. Beat in egg. Add sifted dry ingredients alternately with sour cream, and beat until smooth.

Drop rounded teaspoonfuls onto greased cookie sheets (spaced, they spread). Sprinkle with cinnamon-sugar mixture (use a shaker). Bake in 375° oven for 15 minutes
Yield: 5 dozen 2 inch cookies

CORN FLAKE MACAROONS

1 egg white beaten stiff
1/2 cup sugar
1/2 cup shredded coconut
1 cup corn flakes
1/4 tsp. almond extract
1/4 tsp. vanilla

Mix in order given. Drop from tip of spoon on greased sheet and bake at 375° until brown.

HAMANTASCHEN (PURIM COOKIES)

Dough

1 lb. sweet butter
4 to 4-1/2 cups unsifted all-purpose flour
1 (8 oz.) pkg. cream cheese, softened
1 pint sour cream
2 Tbs. sugar
1 tsp. salt

Cheese Filling

1/2 lb. dry fine-curd cottage cheese, put through a sieve
1 egg, beaten
1/2 cup sugar
1 tsp. vanilla

Poppy-Seed Filling

1/2 lb. ground poppy seed (buy it ground)
1 cup milk
1 cup sugar or 3/4 cup honey
Vanilla, if desired

To make dough:
Make it the day before and chill overnight, if you have time. Work butter and flour together until crumbly. Stir in softened cream cheese and salt. (If necessary, add a little more flour.) Wrap and chill.

Cheese Filling:
Combine all ingredients.

Poppy Seed Filling:
Combine ground poppy seed, milk and sugar or honey in saucepan. Bring just to boiling over very, very, very low heat. Stir in vanilla. Remove from heat.

To form Hamantaschen:
Roll out dough about 1/4 inch thick or a little thinner. Drop filling by the teaspoonful on half the dough, about 2 inches apart.

Fold over other half of dough and cut triangles through both layers. Pinch sides of each cookie together. Scraps of dough can be reworked without getting tough.

Bake at 350° for 20 to 25 minutes.
Yield: 4 dozen

OATMEAL COOKIES

1-1/4 cups butter or margarine, softened
3/4 cup firmly packed brown sugar
1/2 cup sugar
1 large egg
1 teaspoon vanilla extract
1-1/2 cups all-purpose flour
1 tsp. baking soda
1/4 tsp. salt
1 tsp. ground cinnamon
1/4 tsp. ground nutmeg
3 cups regular oats, uncooked
1/2 cup currants or raisins

Beat butter at medium speed with an electric mixer. Gradually add sugars, beating well. Add egg and vanilla; mix well.

Combine flour and next 4 ingredients; gradually add to butter mixture, mixing well. Stir in oats and currants.

Drop dough by tablespoonfuls onto ungreased cookie sheets. Bake at 375° for 10 minutes or until lightly browned. Cool slightly on cookie sheets; remove to wire racks to cool completely.

Yield: 4 dozen

MOM SCHNEIDER'S SCANDINAVIAN COOKIES

1/4 cup confectioner's sugar
1/2 cup shortening (half butter is better)
Yolk of one egg
1 cup all-purpose flour

Mix all ingredients in order given and form into little balls the size of walnuts. Roll these in slightly beaten egg white and then in chopped walnut meats. Place about two inches apart on greased cookie sheet. Make a depression in each cookie with your thumb. Bake at 350° about 12 to 15 minutes. Cool on rack. Before serving, fill the depression in each cookie with currant jelly. They sparkle like little red jewels and guests will love them.

Yield: 3 dozen

Note:
1/4 lb. nuts grated can be added.

BLIZZARD COOKIES

1 cup shortening (solid vegetable shortening or margarine)
1/2 tsp. salt
1 tsp. baking soda
1 cup chunky peanut butter
1 cup sugar
1 cup packed brown sugar
2 well beaten eggs
2 cups all-purpose flour
1 (12 oz.) pkg. chocolate chips

Combine first seven ingredients and mix thoroughly. Add the flour and mix until almost blended, stir in chocolate chips and mix. Cover and chill.

Drop by teaspoons onto an ungreased cookie sheet, press down tops slightly with back of floured spoon or with fingertip. Bake in preheated 325° oven for 8 minutes or until lightly browned. Remove with spatula to cooking rack.

LORI'S PRACTICALLY PERFECT COOKIE

2-1/4 cups flour
1 tsp. baking soda
1 tsp. salt
3/4 cup sugar
3/4 cup brown sugar
2 sticks sweet butter at room temperature
1 tsp. vanilla

2 large eggs
1 (12 oz.) pkg. chocolate chips

Preheat oven to 375°. Mix flour, baking soda and salt in a bowl. Set aside.

Using a standard mixer, mix the two sugars at low speed. Add the butter in small amounts mixing first at low speed then at high speed. Beat until pale, light and very fluffy.

Add vanilla at low speed, then beat on high for a few seconds. Add eggs at lowest speed then high for a second. Mix should look creamed.

Add flour, baking soda and salt, one-half cup at a time, mixing on low speed for a few seconds.

Add chips at low speed for 10 seconds.

Bake on ungreased cookie sheet for 9 to 10 minutes.

Bake at 350° for 12 minutes.
Yield: 3 dozen

Note:
If making chocolate cookies, use 1/2 cup powder or 5 squares, melted.

QUICK MANDEL BREAD COOKIES

3 eggs
1/2 tsp. salt
1/2 cup sugar
2 tsp. cinnamon
1/2 cup oil (scant)
1 cup slivered almonds
1-1/4 cup all-purpose flour
1 tsp. vanilla or almond
   extract
1 tsp. baking powder

Sift together flour, salt, baking powder and cinnamon. Beat eggs until light and lemon colored. Add sugar gradually and beat until thick. Add oil and beat well. Spoon out on greased cookie sheet (with sides up) and bake at 350° for 20 to 25 minutes or until done. Cut into slices and put back into oven to dry at 300° for 15 to 20 minutes.

MANDEL BREAD COOKIES

1/4 lb. butter
1 tsp. vanilla or almond
   extract
1 cup sugar (scant)
2-1/4 cup sifted flour
2 eggs, slightly beaten
1/2 tsp. baking powder
1 tsp. vanilla
1/2 cup chopped nuts

Mix all ingredients together. Grease cookie sheet. Separate dough into 4 loaves. Refrigerate dough overnight. Next day, flatten loaves.

Bake at 360° for 35 to 40 minutes. Slice diagonally while warm, put back in oven if preferred to toast slightly.

Note:
Dough may be frozen for later use.

RUGELACH

1/2 lb. sweet butter
3 egg yolks, beaten
8 oz. softened cream cheese
1 tsp. vanilla
1/2 cup sugar
2 cups flour

Mix all ingredients, make dough. Roll in ball and refrigerate in waxed paper overnight.

Next day, use:
White raisins
Walnuts, crushed
Jam (peach or apricot)
Lemon rind, grated

Roll out dough. Put ingredients around edge (in triangle). Roll up. Place in buttered baking pan.
Bake at 375° until slightly browned. When cool, cut into pieces.

RUGGALACH

4 cups sifted flour
2 eggs
1 pkg. yeast
1 cup milk
1 cup Crisco
1/2 cup warm water
1 cup sugar
2 tsp. sugar

To 1/2 cup warm water, add 2 tsp. sugar and package of yeast. Allow to stand about 10 minutes for yeast to revitalize. Add flour, Crisco, sugar and eggs, plus milk slightly warmed. Mix all together well and allow to stand for 2 hours.

Mix cinnamon and sugar together and chopped nuts. (either walnuts or pecans). Divide risen yeast dough into 6 parts. Work each piece separately on lightly floured board. Roll one section out with rolling pin liberally coated with shortening. Sprinkle with sugar and cinnamon mixture. Sprinkle with nuts. Cut in radial slices about 1-1/2 inches at outer edge. Roll each slice separately. Place on greased cookie sheet in rows.

Bake at 350° for about 35 minutes until light brown.

POSITIVELY-THE-ABSOLUTE-BEST CHOCOLATE-CHIP COOKIES

3/4 cup light brown sugar, firmly packed
2 sticks sweet butter
1 tsp. salt
2-1/4 cups unsifted all-purpose flour
1 tsp. vanilla extract
1 tsp. baking soda
2 cups (12 oz.) semi-sweet chocolate morsels
1 tsp. hot water
3/4 cup granulated sugar
8 oz. (2 generous cups) walnuts, cut or broken into medium-size pieces
2 eggs (large or extra large)

Adjust two racks to divide the oven into thirds and preheat oven to 375°. Cut aluminum foil to fit cookie sheet.

In a large electric mixing bowl, cream the butter. Add salt, vanilla and both sugars; beat well. Add eggs; beat well. On low speed add about half of the flour and, scraping the bowl with a rubber spatula, beat only until incorporated. In a small cup stir the baking soda into the hot water to dissolve it, then mix it into the dough. Add the remaining flour and beat only to mix.

Remove the bowl from the mixer and stir in the walnuts and the morsels.

Although this dough can be, and usually is, simply dropped from a teaspoon, the cookies are much better if you roll the dough between your hands into balls. The cookies will have a more even shape and a more even color.

Spread out a large piece of wax paper on the counter next to the sink. Use a rounded teaspoonful of the dough for each cookie and place the mounds on the wax paper. Then wet your hands with cold water, shake off excess water but do not dry your hands. Pick up a mound of dough and roll it between your wet hands into a smooth, round shape, then press it between your hands to flatten it evenly into a round shape about 1/2 inch thick and place it on the foil. If you refrigerate the dough overnight, it is not necessary to wet your hands; just roll a mound of dough between your hands, flatten it, and place it on the foil. And if you do not refrigerate the dough and do not roll it between your hands but simply drop it from a teaspoon, at least flatten the mounds by pressing them with the back of a wet teaspoon.) Place the flattened rounds of dough 2 inches apart on the foil.

Slide a cookie sheet under the foil and bake 2 sheets at a time, reversing the sheets top to bottom and front to back as necessary during baking to insure even browning. Bake for about 12 minutes or a little longer until the cookies are browned all over. (If you bake only one sheet at a time, bake it on the upper rack.) They must be crisp, - do not underbake.

Let cookies cool for a few seconds on the foil until they are firm enough to be moved. Then, with a wide metal spatula, transfer them to racks to cool. Store airtight.
Yield: 55 (3 inch) cookies

GIANT CHOCOLATE CHIP COOKIES

2 pkgs. (12 oz.) chocolate chips
1 tsp. baking soda
1 tsp. hot water
3/4 cup packed light brown sugar
3/4 sup sugar
1 cup butter
2 eggs, beaten
1 cup chopped walnuts
2-1/4 cup sifted flour
1 tsp. vanilla
1 tsp. salt
1 tsp. butter

In large bowl of electric mixer, at medium speed, cream 1 cup butter until light. Gradually beat in sugars, then eggs, beating until very light and fluffy.

Sift flour mixture with salt. Dissolve baking soda in hot water. Add flour mixture to butter mixture alternately with soda. Set aside 1/4 cup chocolate chips for glaze. Stir in rest of chocolate, nuts and vanilla. Refrigerate dough, covered, overnight.

Preheat oven to 375°. Lightly grease several cookie sheets.

Between palm of hands, roll 1/3 cup dough to form a ball; place 2 or 3 balls on each cookie sheet. Press flat with fingertips to make a 5 inch round.

Bake 10 to 12 minutes or until golden brown. Remove to rack to cool. Continue with rest of dough.

Place 1/4 cup chocolate chips and 1 tsp. butter in small measuring cup set in pan of hot water to melt. Mix well; drizzle over cookies. Allow to cool until chocolate is firm.

CHOCOLATE CHIP COOKIES

1 cup & 2 Tbs. flour
1/2 cup butter, softened
6 Tbs. sugar
1/2 tsp. baking soda
6 Tbs. brown sugar
1/2 tsp. salt
1/2 tsp. vanilla
1/2 cup chopped nuts
1/4 tsp. water
1 cup chocolate chips
1 egg

Cream butter and sugars. Stir in egg. Add vanilla and water. Sift together flour, baking soda and salt. Stir into sugar mixture. Add nuts and chocolate chips. Mix well.

Drop by half-teaspoonfuls on ungreased baking sheet. Bake 10 to 12 minutes at 375°.

NESTLES' CHOCOLATE CHIP COOKIES

3/4 cup firmly packed brown sugar
1 tsp. vanilla
2-1/4 cups unsifted flour
1 tsp. baking soda
1 pkg. chocolate chips
1 tsp. salt
1 cup chopped nuts
1 cup shortening
3/4 cup sugar
2 eggs

Preheat oven to 375°. In small bowl, combine flour, soda and salt; set aside. In large bowl, combine shortening, sugar and vanilla. Beat until creamy. Beat in eggs. Gradually add flour mixture; mix well. Stir in chocolate chips and nuts.

Drop by rounded teaspoonfuls on ungreased cookie sheets. Bake 8 to 10 minutes.

M & M COOKIES

1 pkg. (16 oz.) M & M's
3/4 cup sugar
3/4 cup light brown sugar
2-1/2 cups flour
1/2 tsp. baking soda
2 eggs
1/2 tsp. salt
1 tsp. vanilla
1 cup butter

Preheat oven to 350°. Grease baking sheets. Coarsely chop 1-1/2 cups M & M's. Reserve the rest.

Stir together flour, baking soda and salt. In large bowl, cream butter and sugars. Add eggs and vanilla. Beat until fluffy. Add dry ingredients and chopped candies. Drop by teaspoonfuls on baking sheets. Bake 6 to 7 minutes. Decorate with remaining M & M's.

OLD FASHIONED SUGAR COOKIES

1 cup confectioner's sugar
1 cup butter, softened
1 cup granulated sugar
2 eggs
1 cup melted shortening
2 tsp. vanilla
1 tsp. grated lemon peel
4-1/4 cups flour
1 tsp. cream of tartar
1 tsp. baking soda
1 tsp. salt
Colored sugar for decoration

In large mixing bowl with mixer at medium speed, cream butter and both sugars. Beat in eggs, one at a time until light and fluffy. Add shortening, vanilla and lemon peel. Beat until well mixed. In large bowl, combine flour, baking soda, cream of tartar and salt. Gradually add dry ingredients to creamed mixture; beat until well blended. Wrap and chill dough for several hours.

Preheat oven to 325°. Grease 2 large cookie sheets. Divide dough into thirds. Form heaping teaspoonfuls of dough into balls. Place on cookie sheet. Flatten to a 2 inch diameter with bottom of glass dipped in granulated sugar. Sprinkle with colored sugar. Bake 8 to 10 minutes. Let stand on baking sheet for 2 to 3 minutes before removing.

GIANT SNICKERDOODLES

1-1/2 cups sugar
1 cup butter, softened
2 eggs
2-3/4 cups flour
2 tsp. cream of tartar
1 tsp. baking soda
1/4 tsp. salt
2 tsp. cinnamon
2 Tbs. sugar

In large bowl at medium speed, cream butter 1-1/2 cups sugar and eggs until light and fluffy. In a separate bowl, combine flour, cream of tartar, baking soda and salt. Add to cream mixture until well blended. Refrigerate 30 minutes. Preheat oven to 375°. Combine remaining 2 Tbs. sugar and cinnamon-sugar mixture. Place 3 inches apart on ungreased cookie sheets. Bake 12 to 15 minutes. Cool in rack.

MERINGUE COOKIES

2 egg whites, room temperature
1/8 tsp. salt
1/8 tsp. cream of tartar
3/4 cup sugar

1/2 tsp. vanilla
1 cup chocolate chips
3 Tbs. crushed candy cane
1 cup chopped nuts

Heat oven to 250°. Beat egg whites at high speed in small bowl until foamy. Add salt and cream of tartar. Continue beating until soft peaks form. Add sugar, 1 Tbs. at a time, beating well after each addition. When meringue is stiff and white, add the rest of the ingredients.

Drop by teaspoonfuls about 1-1/2 inches apart onto lightly greased cookie sheet.

Bake 40 minutes. Remove to wire rack to cool

Yield: 5 dozen

TWO STAR CHRISTMAS COOKIES

2/3 cup shortening
4 tsp. milk
3/4 cup sugar
2 cups flour
1 tsp. vanilla
1-1/2 tsp. baking powder
1 egg
1/4 tsp. salt

Thoroughly cream shortening, sugar and vanilla. Add egg and beat until light and fluffy. Stir in milk. Sift together dry ingredients and blend into creamed mixture. Divide dough in half. Chill 1 hour.

On lightly floured surface, roll dough to 1/8 inch thick-

ness. Cut with cookie cutters. Bake on greased cookie sheet for 6 to 8 minutes at 375°. Cool slightly before removing from pan. Cool on rack.

Freezes well. Decorate before baking if not using frosting.

MAGIC PARTY COOKIES

3 cups sifted flour
1 Tbs. baking powder
3/4 tsp. salt
3/4 cup melted butter
2 eggs
1 tsp. vanilla
1 can (15 oz.) Eagle Brand milk
1-1/2 cups cornflakes
1 cup chocolate chips
1/2 cup chopped nuts

Sift together flour, baking powder and salt into a large bowl. Add remaining ingredients and blend thoroughly with an electric mixer. Add chopped nuts (1 or 2) to the center of each cookie when it is placed on baking sheet.

Drop by tablespoonfuls onto well-greased baking sheet. Bake at 350° for about 8 to 10 minutes or until delicately browned around edges. Remove cookies from baking sheet immediately.

Yield: 4 dozen.

CANDY KISS - PEANUT BUTTER COOKIES

1/2 cup shortening
1-3/4 cups flour
1 tsp. baking soda
1/2 cup peanut butter, smooth
1/2 cup sugar
1 egg
1/2 cup brown sugar
2 Tbs. milk
48 candy kisses, unwrapped
1 tsp. vanilla

Preheat oven to 375°. Combine all ingredients except candy kisses in large mixing bowl. Mix on lowest speed until dough forms. Shape dough into balls, using rounded teaspoonfuls for each cookie. Roll ball in sugar and place on ungreased cookie sheets. Bake at 375° for 10 to 12 minutes. Top each cookie immediately with a candy kiss. Press down firmly so cookie cracks around edge.

PEANUT BUTTER COOKIES

1/2 cup shortening
2-1/2 cups flour
1 stick butter
1 tsp. baking powder
1 cup peanut butter, chunky
1-1/2 tsp. baking soda
1 cup sugar
1 cup brown sugar
1 cup salted peanuts, chopped
2 eggs, beaten

Cream together shortening, butter, peanut butter and both sugars. Add eggs, mixing thoroughly. Sift together flour, baking powder and baking soda. Stir the flour mixture into the shortening mixture and chill the dough. Shape dough into small balls and roll in peanuts. Place on greased baking sheet and flatten each ball with a criss-cross made with a fork dipped in flour. Bake at 375° for 10 minutes.

Yield: 6 dozen

PEANUT BUTTER LOGS

1 (15 oz.) Eagle's Brand milk
2 cups sifted flour
2/3 cup peanut butter
2 tsp. baking powder
1/2 cup chopped peanuts
1/2 tsp. salt
1 egg, slightly beaten
1 tsp. vanilla

Stir together flour, baking powder and salt; set aside. Cream peanut butter and egg, using electric mixer. Stir in 1/2 can milk. Blend in half dry ingredients; repeat. Stir in vanilla and nuts. Use 1 tsp. dough to shape into logs. Place on well-greased baking sheet. Bake in 350° about 10 minutes, or until lightly browned. Remove from baking sheet immediately and roll in powdered sugar.

Yield: 8 dozen

120

18 CANDY
& SQUARES

BASIC CHOCOLATE FUDGE

2 oz. unsweetened chocolate, finely chopped
2/3 cups half-and-half
2 cups sugar, sifted
2 Tbs. light corn syrup
1/8 tsp. salt
2 Tbs. unsalted butter
1 tsp. vanilla

Lightly butter the bottom and sides of an 8 inch square baking pan. Lightly butter the sides of a heavy medium saucepan. Add the chocolate and half-and-half. Cook over low heat, stirring constantly for about 5 minutes, until the mixture is smooth.

Stir in the sugar, corn syrup and salt. Continue stirring over low heat for almost 10 minutes, or until the sugar is dissolved. You should not be able to feel the sugar crystals when you rub the spoon against the sides of the saucepan.

Remove the pan from heat and with a damp paper or cloth towel, wipe off the sugar crystals which may have formed above the liquid.

Heat the syrup to boiling and attach a candy thermometer so that it does not touch the bottom of the pan. Cook the syrup over medium heat for about 4 minutes without stirring, until the thermometer registers 238°.

Remove the pan from the heat and add the butter. Cool for about 30 minutes without stirring until lukewarm (110°).

Add the vanilla and beat the fudge vigorously with a wooden spoon for about 2 to 4 minutes until the fudge begins to thicken and lose it's gloss. Quickly spread the fudge into a prepared pan. Let it sit at cool room temperature for about 2 hours until firm. Cut the fudge into 1 inch squares. Store in airtight container at room temperature.

MICROWAVE CHOCO-CARAMEL NUT CANDIES

14 oz. pkg. vanilla caramels
2 Tbs. whipping cream
1 cup chopped pecans
1/2 cup semi-sweet chocolate chips
3 oz. chocolate-flavored candy coating

Line 2 cookie sheets with waxed paper; lightly grease. In 2 quart microwave-safe bowl combine caramels and whipping cream. Microwave on High for 3 to 4 minutes or until melted, stirring after each minute. Stir until smooth. Stir in pecans. To form candies, drop mixture by teaspoonfuls onto prepared cookie sheets, forming 1-1/2 inch circles. Refrigerate to set.

In small microwave-safe bowl, combine chocolate chips and chocolate coating. Microwave on High for 1-1/2 to 2 minutes or until melted, stirring once. Stir until smooth. Dip caramel pecan candies into chocolate mixture; shake off excess. Place on prepared cookie sheets. Refrigerate until set.

Store in airtight container in cool place. May be frozen.

Yield: 40 candies

MICROWAVE CHUNKY PEANUT BUTTER CUPS

Filling
3/4 cup chunky peanut butter
1/2 cup powdered sugar

Coating
1-1/2 cups chocolate chips
9 oz. chocolate candy coating
2/3 cup chunky peanut butter
Miniature paper baking cups (1 inch)

In small bowl, combine 3/4 cup peanut butter and powdered sugar; stir until mixture forms a ball. Cover and refrigerate 1 hour. Using 1/2 tsp. of mixture, shape into balls.

In medium bowl, microwave chocolate chips and chocolate coating on Medium for 4 to 5 minutes, stirring twice. Stir until smooth. Add 2/3 cup peanut butter; blend well. Place

about 1/2 tsp. of chocolate-peanut butter mixture in each paper cup; top each with peanut butter ball. Fill baking cups with remaining chocolate-peanut butter mixture. (If mixture becomes too stiff, microwave on medium 20 to 30 seconds to soften.)

Refrigerate 1/2 hour or until set.

Yield: 6 dozen

HEAVENLY HASH

1 lb. semi-sweet chocolate
2 capfuls vanilla
2 Tbs. wax (paraffin)
2/3 bar butter

Use double boiler:

Mix well until all ingredients are melted. Add chopped nuts.

Grease cookie sheet. Take fork and dip marshmallows in above ingredients. Let cool.

CHOCOLATE FUDGE I

2 squares unsweetened chocolate
1/4 cup chopped nuts
1 pkg. (3 oz.) cream cheese
1/4 tsp. vanilla
2 cups sifted powdered sugar
Dash of salt

Cream cheese with wooden spoon. Blend in sugar. Melt chocolate over hot water. Add chocolate and blend well. Add vanilla, salt and nuts. Blend thoroughly. Grease shallow pan and press

fudge into it. Place in refrigerator until firm. Cut into squares.

CHOCOLATE FUDGE II

1/3 cup cocoa
2 cups sugar
3/4 cup scalded milk
3 Tbs. butter
1 tsp. light corn syrup
1 tsp. vanilla

Add sugar, corn syrup to milk, stirring until sugar dissolves. Cook gently to soft ball stage — 234° to 238°. Stir frequently.

Remove from heat. Add butter and cool to room temperature or 110° without stirring. Add vanilla. Beat until thick and looses its gloss. Spread quickly.

CHOCOLATE FUDGE III

1 pkg. (3 oz.) cream cheese
1/4 tsp. vanilla
2 squares unsweetened chocolate
1/4 cup chopped nuts
2 cups sifted confectioner's sugar
Dash of salt
Butter

Cream cheese with wooden spoon. Blend in sugar. Melt chocolate over hot water. Add chocolate and blend well. Add vanilla, salt, and nuts. Blend thoroughly.

Grease shallow pan and press fudge into it. Place in refrigerator until firm. Cut into squares.

THE BEST CHOCOLATE FUDGE IV

3 squares unsweetened chocolate
3 cups sugar
2 Tbs. light corn syrup
1 cup milk
3 Tbs. butter or margarine
1/2 tsp. salt
1 cups pecans, coarsely chopped
1-1/2 tsp. vanilla extract

About 2-1/2 hours before serving or up to 1 week ahead:

In 4 quart saucepan over medium heat, heat sugar, milk, chocolate, corn syrup, and salt to boiling, stirring frequently. Carefully set candy thermometer in place and cook, without stirring, until temperature on thermometer reaches 238° or soft-ball stage (when a small amount of chocolate mixture dropped into a bowl of very cold water forms a ball that flattens on removal from water), about 10 minutes. Remove saucepan from heat.

Cool chocolate mixture, without stirring, to 110°, or until outside of saucepan is lukewarm. Meanwhile, lightly butter 8 inch square baking pan.

When chocolate mixture is ready, add butter or margarine and vanilla extract. With wooden spoon, beat until mixture is thick and begins to lose its gloss, about 3 minutes. Quickly stir in chopped pecans; pour mixture into pan. Cool fudge in pan on wire rack; cut into about 1-1/2 inch squares. Store fudge in tightly covered container.

Yield: 2 lbs. or 25 pieces

Note:

Old-fashioned fudge is a chocolate-lover's dream. It's easy to create that velvety melt-in-your-mouth texture batch after batch.

The trick to perfect fudge is to cook the chocolate mixture to precisely the correct temperature. Undercooking creates fudge that is too soft; overcooking will harden the fudge.

A candy thermometer will eliminate any guesswork. Be sure to insert it at least 2 inches deep into the chocolate mixture - the chocolate will bubble up in the saucepan as it boils.

Remove the chocolate from the heat precisely at the "softball" stage, 238°. You can also test the mixture by dropping a small amount into very cold water. If the chocolate has cooked sufficiently, it will clump together into a soft mass that can be shaped with your fingers. When the fudge has cooled to lukewarm (110°), beat it just until it begins to look less glossy.

Overbeating will harden the fudge.

FOOLPROOF CHOCOLATE FUDGE V

3 pkgs. (6 oz.) chocolate chips
1-1/2 tsp. vanilla
1 can (14 oz.) Eagle Brand sweetened milk
1/2 cup chopped nuts (optional)
Dash of salt

In heavy saucepan, over low heat, melt chocolate with milk. Remove from heat; stir in remaining ingredients. Spread evenly into wax paper-lined 8 inch square pan. Chill 2 hours. Turn fudge onto cutting board; peel off paper and cut into squares. Cover and store at room temperature.

Peanut Butter: Omit chocolate chips, vanilla and nuts. In heavy saucepan, melt 1 pkg. (12 oz.) peanut butter flavored chips. Remove from heat; stir in sweetened condensed milk and dash of salt. Proceed as directed.

CHOCOLATE MARSHMALLOW FUDGE SUPREME VI

1 pkg. (8 oz.) chocolate chips
1 Tbs. butter
1-1/2 cups miniature marsh-
    mallows
1-2/3 cups sugar
2/3 cup evaporated milk
1/2 cup chopped nuts
    (optional)
1/4 tsp. salt

Break chocolate into pieces and place in mixing bowl. Add marshmallows, and nuts if desired, butter and vanilla; set aside. Combine sugar, milk and salt in 2 quart saucepan. Stir constantly over medium heat until mixture comes to a full boil. Boil and stir for 3 minutes or 225° with candy thermometer. Pour hot syrup over ingredients in mixing bowl, stir until marshmallow and chocolate are completely melted. Pour into buttered 8 or 9 inch pan. Cool. Cut.

CHOCOLATE FUDGE VII

2 squares unsweetened
    chocolate
1/8 tsp. salt
2/3 cup milk
2 Tbs. butter
2 cups sugar
1 tsp. vanilla

Break chocolate into small pieces. Add to milk in saucepan. Cook over low heat, stirring constantly until mixture is smooth. Add sugar, salt and stir until sugar is dissolved and mixture boils. Cook slowly without stirring, until a small quantity dropped into cold water forms a soft ball. Remove from heat. Add butter and vanilla without stirring. Cool to lukewarm. Beat until fairly thick. Pour at once into greased pan. Cool. Cut.

FIVE STAR FUDGE VIII

1 jar (5 to 10 oz.) marshmal-
    low creme
1/4 tsp. salt
2/3 cup evaporated milk
1/4 cup butter
1-1/2 cup sugar
1 tsp. vanilla
2 pkgs. chocolate chips

Combine marshmallow cream, milk, butter, sugar and salt in saucepan. Stir over moderate heat until mixture comes to a full rolling boil. Boil 5 minutes, stirring constantly. Add chocolate chips and vanilla. Stir until smooth. Turn into greased 8 or 9 inch square pan. Chill until firm. Cut into squares.

CHOCOLATE FUDGE IX

2 oz. unsweetened chocolate
1 tsp. corn syrup
2 cups sugar
2 Tbs. butter
3/4 cup milk
1 tsp. vanilla
Dash of salt

Butter sides of 2 or 3 quart saucepan. Combine sugar, milk, chocolate, salt and corn syrup. Heat and stir over medium heat until sugar dissolves and mixture comes to a boil (238°). Do not stir while mixture is cooking unless necessary. Add butter and let cool to lukewarm (110°) without stirring.

The pot should be cool to touch. Add vanilla and beat vigorously. Soon mixture will become very thick and will start to lose its gloss. Pour into buttered shallow pan.

Variation:

Pour mixture onto buttered board and knead like dough. Roll in logs. Wrap in wax paper and chill. Slice like cookies.

CARAMEL

1 cup brown sugar
2 cups sugar
2/3 cup light corn syrup
2/3 cup butter
1 cup cream
2 tsp. vanilla
1 tsp. salt

Mix ingredients together in deep 2 quart saucepan.

Cook to 246° stirring constantly toward end of cooking period to prevent scorching.

CANDY APPLES ON A STICK

8 medium-size red apples
1 cup water
1/2 tsp. cinnamon flavoring
2 cups sugar
2/3 cup light corn syrup
Red food coloring

Select firm, red apples. Wash and polish.

Grease cookie sheet lightly. Remove stems from washed and polished apples. Insert wooden sticks firmly in stem end.

Stir sugar, syrup and water together in medium-size saucepan over moderate heat until sugar almost dissolves. Cover pan and bring slowly to a boil. Remove cover and boil rapidly without stirring until 1 tsp. of syrup dropped into cold water separates into hard, brittle threads or registers 300° on candy thermometer.

During cooking, wipe inside of pan often with wet cheesecloth wrapped around a fork. At 300° add flavoring and enough coloring to tint syrup bright red. Remove at once from heat. Stir only until color is evenly distributed.

Tip saucepan. Dip apples, twisting in syrup until covered. Let extra syrup on apples drain back into saucepan. Work quickly, placing saucepan over boiling water if necessary to keep syrup thin enough to coat apples easily. Save any excess syrup to help stick decorations on applies. Place coated apples stick up, on prepared cookie sheet to harden.

MOLASSES TAFFY

2 cups sugar
2 tsp. vinegar
1 cup light molasses
2 Tbs. butter
1/3 cup water
1/2 tsp. soda

Butter sides of heavy 2 quart saucepan. Combine sugar, molasses and water. Heat slowly and stir until all sugar is dissolved.

Bring to boiling and add vinegar. Cook to light crack stage (268°).

Remove from heat; add butter and sift in soda, stir to mix. Turn into large shallow buttered pan - don't scrape sides of cooling pan! Use a spatula to turn edges of candy to center so candy cools evenly.

As soon as it is cool enough to handle, pull the taffy. The hotter it can be handled, the better. When taffy changes from brown to light golden color and gets hard to pull, cut in fourths. Pull each piece into a long strand. Cut into bite-size pieces, using scissors dipped in butter. When cold wrap each piece in wax paper.

THE WORLD'S BEST CARAMEL CANDY

2 cups heavy cream, heated to lukewarm
2 cups sugar
1 cup light corn syrup.
1/4 tsp. salt
1 tsp. vanilla
1/4 cup butter

In deep saucepan, mix sugar and syrup. Stir until sugar dissolves and mixture boils. Cook to 270° on a candy thermometer without stirring.

Slowly add 1 cup warm cream while mixture never stops boiling. Cook to 250° stirring frequently. Carefully add remaining cup cream, 1 Tbs. at a time, stirring constantly. Now add salt and butter. Cook to 250° stirring if necessary.

Remove from heat. Add vanilla. Pour into buttered 9 inch square pan. Mark in squares, but do not cut through. When cool, turn out on a board and cut into squares. Wrap each piece in plastic wrap.

MARSHMALLOWS

1/3 cup confectioner's sugar
1/4 cup cornstarch
1 envelope unflavored gelatin
1/3 cup water
1/2 cup light corn syrup
1 tsp. vanilla
2/3 cup granulated sugar
1/4 tsp. salt

Sift together the cornstarch and confectioner's sugar. Lightly butter an 8 inch square baking pan and sprinkle with 1 Tbs. of the cornstarch mixture. Tilt pan in all directions to coat bottom and sides. Do not shake out excess.

Blend the gelatin and water in a small saucepan and let soak. Add the granulated sugar and stir over low heat until gelatin and sugar dissolves. In the bowl of an electric mixer, combine the gelatin mixture, corn syrup, salt and vanilla. Beat 15 minutes on high speed until peaks form. Spread the gelatin mixture over the bottom of the prepared pan and smooth the top. Let stand 2 hours or until well set.

With a wet knife, cut the marshmallow mixture into quarters and loosen around the edges. Sprinkle remaining cornstarch on a baking sheet and invert the marshmallows onto it. Cut each quarter into 9 pieces and roll each in the cornstarch and sugar mixture. Place the marshmallow on a rack and cover with paper towels. Let stand overnight to dry the surface slightly.

RICE KRISPIES MARSHMALLOW TREATS

1 pkg. (10 oz.) marshmallows or 4 cups miniature marshmallows
1/4 cup butter
5 cups Rice Krispies

Melt butter in large saucepan over low heat. Add marshmallows and stir until melted and well blended. Remove from heat. Add Rice Krispies cereal. Stir until well coated. Press mixture evenly into greased 13 x 9 x 2 inch pan. Cool completely.

Yield: 24 squares (each 2 inch square)

Variations:

Peanut Butter: Stir 1/4 cup peanut butter into marshmallow mixture just before adding Rice Krispies.

Peppermint: Add 1/2 cup crushed peppermint candy with cereal. Other hard candies may be used.

Raisin: Add 1 cup raisins with Rice Krispies cereal.

S'MORES

2/3 cup light corn syrup
1 tsp. vanilla
1 pkg. (8 cups) Golden Grahams
2 Tbs. butter
3 cups mini marshmallows
1 pkg. chocolate chips

Grease 13 x 9 x 2 inch rectangular pan. Heat corn syrup, butter and chocolate chips to boiling in 3 quart saucepan, stirring constantly; remove from heat. Stir in vanilla. Pour over cereal in large mixing bowl, toss quickly until completely coated. Fold in marshmallows, 1 cup at a time. Press mixture evenly in pan with wax paper. Let stand 1 hour.

Yield: 48 squares

19 SPECIAL IDEAS
& HINTS

HOMEMADE CHRISTMAS ORNAMENTS

(NOT TO BE EATEN)
1/2 cup flour
1/2 cup salt
1/4 cup water

Roll and cut with cookie cutters. Poke hole with pin for hanging. Let dry for 24 hours, then paint and decorate.

SALT SCULPTURE DOUGH

(NOT TO BE EATEN)
2 cups flour (not self-rising)
1 cup salt
1 cup water

Combine flour and salt in a large flat-bottomed bowl, and mix well with spoon. Next, add water (a little at a time) mixing as you pour to form the dough into a ball. Additional water may be needed, depending on the humidity. Take care not to add too much so dough becomes sticky.

Knead 7 to 10 minutes until dough has a smooth, yet firm consistency. Place dough that will not be used immediately in a plastic bag to keep it from drying.

Place finished pieces on foil-covered cookie sheet and place in 325° to 350° oven. Allow to bake 30 minutes for each 1/4 inch of thickness, or until golden brown. If sculptures pull up, reduce oven temperature by 50° to 75° and poke piece with pin or toothpick to release air.

SCENTS OF THE HOLIDAYS

(NOT EDIBLE)
In a small saucepan, combine 2 cinnamon sticks, 3 whole cloves, 3 whole allspice and 3 cups of water.

Bring to a boil; reduce heat. Simmer over low heat. Check mixture periodically and add more water if necessary.

Simmer this mixture before guests arrive to fill your home with the "scents of the holidays."

CHILDREN'S PARTIES

Garnish a cake for a boy with miniature cars and trucks around edges. The children may take them home afterward.

For a girl's [arty, make a Chiffon cake and insert a doll in the hole in the center. Garnish the cake with silver decorating balls (dragees).

For a Valentine party, make cake in heart-shaped pans. Ice with a while frosting and make a border outlining the Valentine shape with tiny cinnamon hearts.

Ball Cake: (Good for Halloween party.) Use Pyrex or aluminum bowls instead of regular baking pans when making cake. Make a double recipe, and pour into 2 bowls of equal size. Bake as directed. Put together with icing (flat tops face to face) and frost or ice completely. Perfect to make a jack-o-lantern face, bouncing ball, etc. Decorate appropriately.

If you have no candle holders, use gum drops or life savers instead.

Polka Dot Cake: Ice cake with white frosting. Reserve some, and tint a deep pink. Dip the spoon in tinted icing and make circular indentations here and there over the entire cake. Cute for a little girl's party.

Children's Rainbow Cake: Divide cake batter into 5 parts. Leave one part white, and tint the other 4 parts with food coloring, (red, green, yellow) and cocoa. Spoon colored batters alternately into pan.

Make a party at mealtime, rather than mid-day. The children's appetites will be spoiled for their meal at home anyway.

Cut slits in each slice of cake. Insert coins of different denominations which have been wrapped in plastic wrap or foil.

Ice Cream Cupcakes: Pour cake batter into flat bottom cones. Bake 20 to 25 minutes at 350°. Cool. Mound icing to resemble an ice cream cone. Cones won't brown in the baking.

Party Clowns: Invert cones on a small scoop of ice cream. Make eyes from chocolate chips, mouths from maraschino cherries, noses and ears from jelly beans. Cone hats may be iced, if desired.

Snow Man: Boll a large and small scoop of ice cream in shredded coconut. Place the small ball on top. Use an inverted baking cup as a hat, chocolate chips for eyes, raisins for a nose, cherry for a mouth and a lollipop for a broom.

RECIPES FOR ACTIVITIES OF THE ILL CHILD

Explore the top shelf of the closet for those surplus presents from the last birthday which were put away for just an occasion.

Scrap books can be made from notebooks by pasting in pictures from magazines or old greeting cards.

Using an old catalogue, the child can cut out his "house", putting together all the pictures that show items that go in a kitchen, etc.

A pretty picture can be pasted on cardboard, then cut into pieces to make a puzzle.

Soap bubbles can be blown from an old spool if one end is dipped in soapy water and the child blows through the other end.

If medicine is a problem:
Pills may go down more easily embedded in a jelly sandwich or a maraschino cherry, or crushed in a spoon of applesauce. Liquid medicine sucked through a colored straw is likely to be more fun than when drunk from a cup.

In something really tastes bad, chunks of ice held in the mouth just before and again just after swallowing the bad-tasting medicine deaden the sense of taste.

If food is a problem:
A "picnic" box with small wrapped sandwiches or other surprises may add new appeal to familiar food. Suggestions: Butter a piece of toast and cut in into odd shapes for the patient to fit together jigsaw fashion before eating. A "face" may be made on a slice of buttered toast by sifting a cinnamon and sugar mixture onto it through a stencil and setting it for a moment in a hot oven. Or you may ask your child to guess what he'll find on the bottom of his glass plate when finished with his food. Beforehand, you may paste a funny picture on the under side or draw one yourself with nail polish, if using a paper plate. If your child likes pancakes, try "dollar" size ones that are easily made into animals or that are easy to manipulate in bed. If he likes macaroni and cheese, buy spirals, or sea shells, or wheels, or bowties and add the cheese. The novelty of the food often helps it to disappear fast.